Notes

70% of learning comes from taking notes

Notes

70% of learning comes from taking notes.

Fruition

From Ideas to Reality

Ten Brave Entrepreneurs Share Their Stories and Journey's

Created by
831
Designs
BOOKS

831 DESIGNS UK

831 Designs is part of Forever Family Forever Free group of Companies whose address can be found at 831Designs.com.

First published in the United Kingdom.

This book was created using the You Speak, We Create done for you service at 831 Designs.

Copyright © 2017 by 831Designs

All rights reserved.

No part of these pages, either text or image may be used for any purpose other than personal use. Therefore, reproduction, modification, storage in a retrieval system or retransmission, in any form or by any means, electronic, mechanical or otherwise, for reasons other than personal use, is strictly prohibited without prior written permission.

First published 2017: 831 Designs, London. UK Edited by Mark Kehoe

www.831Designs.com

Book: Fruition

David Herbert. + **Multiple Authors**– 2nd ed.

ISBN-13: 978-1719364539

Foreword

This book was inspired by all the "make money online FAST" videos, "hustle hard for 30-90 days then you will have millions and spend the rest of your life on a beach." It excites me to see people stepping out of their comfort zone and actually going for it, actually trying to create a life on their terms. But it upsets me when after 30-90 days they are giving up and going back to the 9-5, and I believe a lot of this has to do with unrealistic expectations, created by great marketers. I know there will always be that one incredible example, but for most things do not happen in such a short time. Most overnight success took years to create. With this in mind I was inspired to create a book, a reference, some real-life lessons and examples. To show the truth behind the success story. With hope that this will help and inspire more people to try harder, to keep going, to never give up. We have all faced different challenges, but we have overcome them and now we are finally seeing the fruits of our labour! In this book I interview ten incredible and brave entrepreneurs that share the "real truth" behind their journey's, in hope that they can help you on your journey. With ten different perspectives there's bound to be at least one that resonates with you.

My hope is that this shows enough raw truths to keep you pushing through your challenges to create life on your terms. I had so much fun connecting with all of these incredible authors, I hope you have as much fun reading it.

Laura Helen
Best Selling author and creator
AKA Mummy - Forever Family Forever Free

Table of Contents

How Long is Overnight Success 1

Find Your Drive and Jump 19

Relationships and Mindset 35

Misunderstood to Reconnecting the World 79

Impact and Influence 87

Queen of self-love helping you to tap into your inner peace. 97

From Poverty, Drugs & Violence to International Speaker, TV Show Host &Spiritual Teacher 121

Closing of the book. 139

WHY I hate my Kids 142

"May you gather the strength to hold onto your dreams and follow your passion."

1

How Long is Overnight Success

Here we go again, leaving my kids at the front door crying, "Daddy, please don't go" promising that I will see them later, but in the back of my mind, knowing they will probably be asleep by the time I get back home after work and traveling back. Going to a job that I like but it takes me away from my family, takes me away from seeing my children grow, watching them develop.

You hear people say it's easy, "In 3 steps you can be as rich as me" and 30 days to $30K

My journey started eight years ago, Laura and I gave up two full time 90+ hours a week jobs and moved to Cornwall for a chilled-out kind of life.

Having a job to go to and only needing to look for a part-time job for Laura, we moved.

It turns out that the job I was supposed to move to was waiting for a disciplinary action taken against a former employee, which took six weeks, having known that it was going to take six weeks I may have looked for something in the meantime. but being told, "next week," "next week."

We had been working non-stop for eight months, 90+ hours a week, without seeing each other or even the outside for that matter, so we just enjoyed being together. It was Cornwall, June and the weather was fantastic. We had an excellent garden where we spent loads of time, having some chill-out time, BBQs each night, country walks and beaches. There was beautiful little spot two miles from where we lived. It was out of the way from the "tourist," a trek to get to, but beautiful. We were living life on "our terms" we thought!

We had just moved in, so bedding, crockery, cutlery, microwave, washer dryer, towels, things to make a house a home. All this cost money and living like we had the £5,000 savings in the bank that never went down, it was a shock when it started to run out.

I finally got the job which I had come for, great job, high pay, the only thing is, I had to work a month in hand, usual for most employers, but as I started in the middle of the month I had to wait six weeks for my first pay check. 12 weeks, without any pay, this would have been alright, if we hadn't "enjoyed" the holidays so much and spent almost all we had.

From that point, we were playing catch-up, with rent and bills. Laura "having to get a job out of necessity rather than being optional. It was almost Christmas, and we had nothing left. We had £200 for food, decorations, gifts for family and each other.

We were used to much, much more, one year we had a 9-ft. real Christmas tree, with loads of gifts for each other, spoiling family members and having a feast, to this, to struggling. We still made it unique, but deep down I knew Laura deserved more.

January, when I got paid it did not cover the bills, it was January in Cornwall, so, no tourist or passing trade, so the company that I worked for, was slow; hence the bonus was poor, and the paycheck was light. February, we struggled again, we were in trouble.

We were doing all sorts online trying to make an extra few quid. We bought stuff from eBay at random times, sometimes staying up to 3 am to get a deal, where it was listed to finish at the wrong time, searching for incorrect spellings, or scrolling down pages after pages of eBay listings for each category by ending soonest and lowest price to get a deal. After this we would re-list the product back on eBay, with great pictures, catchy titles and a "story" why we were selling it, this made a real difference when selling, people "bought" into this and usually get a much higher price, sometimes, selling it before we even received it. This helped a lot but not enough, we were both growing tired, and by April we considered getting help. We had one last shot at making this work on our own, we bought a 6-week online marketing and coaching course, with an American company called Prosper, we had a couple of calls and saw this as our only answer, assured we would make fast money with all the info we would be getting, we made the payment, $2,200. We bit the bullet, burned the bridges, went all in. After the first week, reading all the info on drop shipping and supplying value and how to make money online, I had my second coaching call, it was decided to set up a website and sell from there, find products and sell directly, but what could I sell I said, "What do you know" he said.

I know cars, tyres, mechanics, that's all I knew, that's what I did, I knew, kitchens as a chef, bars as a bartender, I knew lots in the service industry, but I needed a product to sell.

Tyres, that's a product, and working through the steps to find my ideal customer, where to find and contact suppliers, designing and building the website. NEW TYRES QUICK was born. Clickety Click, New Tyres Quick.

I had a supplier, I had a design, and I had a mission.

It was going great, we knew what we were doing, but it all took time, we were running out of time and in August we eventually got an IVA, a bit like being bankrupt, but we paid as much back as we could a month rather than nothing at all.

This gave us relief with the credit card interest payments, loans not being met and rent being late each month. 2 years earlier, we were high-income earners, we were bringing in £5k+ a month whilst living very minimal bills, we "lived in" with our jobs, our bills were taken out of our wages before we got them, what we got was ours, so to then "fend" for ourselves, we had no idea, how to look after our money, we got it, we had it, we spent it.

The website was being built by a web developer, and I was inputting all the pages and products, over 1000 products with descriptions, images, pricing, and SEO. This all took hours and hours and hours. I wanted this so bad, I just kept working for it, all I had was time, I could sleep on 4 hours a night so that I could get it done.

As the website was built and the business was created, I decided to change jobs, doing the same thing, Mechanics but with a different company. The company I was with, main business was selling tyres and selling tyres online, I thought best to leave now, than later with no warning for being dismissed for "Conflict of interest."

As I started a few weeks in I said that this would not be permanent, as I had an online business and I was waiting to build up to give me the freedom to work from home. Always having that dream of being self-sufficient and having a passive income, never wanting to be an employee working for others, I am too "Hot-headed" I can listen and follow instructions, but if I think I have a better way, I am not afraid to let it be known. After about a year New Tyres Quick was doing about £200 a Month, yes, a Month, and not that consistently. With the IVA in place and New Tyres Quick not moving very fast, we started property investing with no money down deals, as we had no money to put down, but we had the knowledge and determination that could get it done.

Working harder on my life outside of my 9-5 job well 8-6 job, up till midnight - 2.00 some mornings, and making use of my lunch break and time to and from work wisely, researching, making calls, reading and learning new techniques, I certainly used my 24 hours wisely.

I left that job, you might be thinking that I don't stick at anything, you would be very wrong, if I am not happy I WILL change it. I was being shouted at by my boss because he hated his job as much as I hated mine, and he was the owner with no way out.

New job, still Mechanics but hitting properties harder than ever, viewing's after work, property webinars for more in-depth knowledge, meeting with estate agents on my lunch break. Working through my lunch break so that I could leave early to go to networking events.

This all paid off, we got our first property, £300 per month, passive income, we got our second property, cost us £500 a month as we couldn't let it out, and after three months we eventually got rid of it, so cost us £1,500. So, five months of getting the £300 for the first property just to break even.

Then was the time we were helping Tegan publish her first book. We were going to London twice a month to promote her book with events, seminars, and Tegan speaking on stage. We got our third property, a 3-bedroom house, converted to a 5-bedroom HMO (house of multiple occupancies) in the middle of a busy town. This was it; we worked out the figures, should have brought in £1500 a month, shared between a partner and us, so approx. £750 a month. We were halfway there £1050 passive income, work hard once and keep getting paid right. NO, we got totally screwed, we never received £750, any months, as our partner, whom we thought was a friend, was not.

In the meantime, before we knew we were not going to receive any money from the third property, I had an argument with my boss and walked out, I said I was "hot-headed."

We had enough to pay for our expenses, just about, and it gave me more time to really crack on and do what was needed, I was running out of hours when I was working 48 hours a week, so with this extra focus time, I could bring in even more passive income. We had enough for expenses but anything extra such as events, traveling and accommodation to London every other weekend we found we were running out.

It was an amazing time, seeing my children, early in the morning, days out, parks, reading, having meals together, I loved it, we all did as a family.

Money was running out again, and I had a choice, keep on doing what I was doing, working on our own business with a chance of falling behind on our bills again or go back to work. I went back to work. That was one of the hardest decision that I have ever had to make. Hard on the kids, and every morning, asking when are you finishing, why can't you stay at home, we love seeing you, will you be home for dinner? It broke my heart leaving them crying at the front door, wanting me to stay home, but without any money, we were not getting anywhere. We decided to cut our expenses right down; we worked out what would be best Cornwall or London?

Cornwall
  £600 Rent
  £120 Electric
  £40 Internet
  £140 car insurance
  £120 Fuel for car
  £120 Council tax
  £35 Water
  £50 Maintenance of vehicle

£50 Upkeep of house

£200 Trips to London

£1335 per month bills

London

£850 – Accommodation

£150 – Travel Bus and trains

£1000 per month bills

We were saving £300+ a month and had more opportunities.

It seemed viable to move to London and live out of a suitcase so that we could be closer to the action. We had no traveling or accommodation costs to pay for, for events we could go to a one-day networking event, or an evening, which we would never be able to do from Cornwall.

So, we sold a lot of stuff that we could in the time frame, but most of it went to charity shops as we were running out of time and moved to London.

I had a job to go to straight away, transfer with my company, £22k - £28k with the Cornwall / London pay difference, which was great, because we did not carry the London lifestyle with us, we kept it close with a one bedroom flat. We surprisingly found food, and drink cheap, Avocados, Cornwall £1.20 each, London a bowl for a pound, 5-6 for £1, and a phone screen cheap, £75 in Cornwall iPhone5, £35 in London.

I left for work at 7 am and getting back at 7 pm. On the commute, I always had a pen and paper, working on something or other. During work, I had headphones in while working, listening to audiobooks, such as "The Next-Door Millionaire." By the time, I came home, it was 7 pm. The kids would usually be asleep, and I wouldn't see them at all if I were lucky they would still be awake. That was great, I would see them and hear all about their day, and they would get so excited it would be 8 pm before they went down with all the excitement, which was great but, means we got to work at 9 o'clock sometimes, then 3 or 4 hours working on our business, tyre orders, books formatting, editing, coaching calls or networking. Going to bed at one o clock sometimes, to get the work that was time sensitive finished.

One time when we were creating a "Money for Kids" board game, and we had to get it ready for the Ultra kid's club fare at Christmas, we were up till 3 am for three nights in a row to get that completed. Still up at 7 am for work and for Laura to look after the kids.

I DO NOT RECOMMEND DOING THAT FOR TOO MANY NIGHTS.

We usually aim for 6-7 hours of sleep a night.

Sometimes you must Hustle!

As with my journey, it wasn't plain sailing, after two months of being transferred, I did not receive the pay rise that was due to me, so I was losing even more money. Also, we got stung for the tenant deposits, that our property partner never paid, £1500 extra we had to pay along with £3000 in rent that we never got. I changed jobs again, this time for the £28k, plus extra if I work sat mornings for a more chilled out garage.

I was there for about five months, one of the best jobs that I have had, the lads were great, the boss and managers were great, relaxed atmosphere and no pushy sales or targets and I enjoyed the work. I almost felt bad, as he wanted a long-term member of staff and I knew I wasn't going to stay, I missed my wife and kids, seeing photos in messages of them in the park or pool, or dressing up and being creative, that really cut me deep. I loved seeing them but at the same time showing me what I was missing.

When is the right time to go solo?

Employment was not for me, I love to be free, I want to be my own boss, well the wife is, but sometimes she lets me play boss, lol. We worked so closely with each other, and we still are. We worked so hard, for so many years. We had a range of business ventures, some worked, and some did not, but what we did learn was never to give up.

THE HARDEST THING ABOUT BEING AN ENTREPRENEUR IS CASHFLOW.

Some weeks and months went well, we invested in more, books, events, seminars and treated ourselves, some weeks and some months went not so well, and some months dried up completely.

We were moving to different Airbnb's around London, according to events and people we met, after a bad experience we decide to live in a hotel, a new premier inn at Heathrow, new, so super saver rates, and because we booked for a month we got a better deal, the first few weeks were expensive, but then got it down to £850 a month. Then we hit another cashflow incident, and we were paying week by week, ouch.

From £850 a month to £1500 a month, we were not saving anything, almost a month's wage was going to accommodation. Something had to give, looking for accommodation around London, kept coming up with foreign stays.

A crazy plan came together to move abroad; we can stay somewhere hot for a whole month less than £850, less than £600, this was it, we really were cutting down our expenses. But this came with a drawback; I would not be employed, we would not have that guaranteed income (well only the guarantee, if my boss needed me there)

I would have an extra 360 hours to work on ourselves, our businesses, our clients.

We had two books going at the same time and found not having enough time was limiting us from getting any more. We spoke to our children about it, and all agreed,

We were already living out of a suitcase as this was our choice, our way of life; our goal had always been to travel, travel around the world, home-schooling, working from our laptops, speaking as a family and inspiring others.

This was our next chapter, as Forever Family Forever Free. Total freedom, I still get up at 6 am and can have my work done by 8 am, and I am finished, after that, we can go down to the beach, the pool or park and have the family time that we had all been longing for.

Having more time to think and do, has given us multiple ideas to come up with and to do. The kids are enjoying all of us being together, having a dream to work from home has always spurred me on and having a strong enough why, my kids have kept me going, on those dark winter mornings and those very late nights. Multiple streams of income have been something that Laura and I have worked on for many years, building up each business together, laying the foundations with each one.

We still work hard, and we play even harder, we serve even more people with our products and our mission is to provide more value than we take in payment.

All the challenges and gruel and grit that we have encountered over the years have well been worth it and would we do it all over again, hell, yes. Having the family freedom that we have all been yearning for. We are still in the infancy of our journey and are excited with what will unravel over the next five years.

Look out for our journey and connect with us.

David Herbert

www.foreverfamilyforeverfree.com

www.newtyresquick.com

Tegan Helen

Facebook.com/KidsGetLearning

"Lay the foundations to build an empire"

2

Find Your Drive and Jump

I have been in fitness and nutrition ever since I was a kid which is what lead me into starting my own organization called 'Core Capacity Transformations. We currently have 8 locations and have recently become a national franchise. It has been a beautiful journey and I am very grateful and humbled to be a part of it. My name is Trevor Buccieri and I am a life transformational strategist.

My entrepreneurial journey started when I was eleven years old, my father was my greatest mentor. He started a lawn mowing business with me, and we would go together to businesses and mow their lawns for them on the weekends. It was a great way to earn money, even though I wasn't sure what was going on? I knew I enjoyed it and it was very fulfilling to be able to do it and create cash by ourselves. Because I was eleven I was too young to get hired, yet I was able to earn my own money and I kept this business going for several years. After that I worked for several other people at different places from a sub shop, a bike shop and dicks sporting goods store which I found that it really wasn't for me. I was let go from a couple of those jobs, because I didn't do well at following instructions that I didn't agree with.

At that point I had the feeling that this really isn't for me, so I went into education, which was great because I found that I was spending all my time trying to convince the kids that didn't want to learn, that the information that I had to share with them was valuable, as opposed to doing the actual teaching, really helping to change lives in that sense as well. After that I started my own personal training business, as I went into grad school, so I did that on the side, doing one on one training and going to school at the same time. The true start of my entrepreneurial journey, the big turning point was when I found out that my fiancé was pregnant. That really turned something on inside me. It really made me feel that this idea I had in the back of my mind, that I have been too scared to do that, NOW was the time to do it! It really made me jump and it gave me the inspiration to jump. It gave me a greater purpose to start taking action and believing in myself. That was back in 2009 when my true journey started. I started my first larger company, 'Body and Soul Boot Camp the Experience', which is now 'Core Capacity'. That's where it all began. With all the knowledge I have acquired, all the education I have delved into and the personal development that I have really committed to over the last ten years this has lead me to my latest release, my latest launch which is a brand under my own personal name 'Trevor Buccieri', this is an education and coaching company, where I am teaching people all about the mind in conquering their mindset and also their body from an exercise stand point as well as nutrition and bridging that gap with things like mediation, breathing, our heart rhythm, gratitude and rituals. I also delve into business, structures and how to accelerate any area of your business such as an analysis type system, a system of checks and balances if you will, to analyze the health of your business and to also strategize to cover on any area that isn't thriving. These are the things that I've delved into at this point in my career.

Whilst there has been challenges every single day my greatest challenge throughout this journey which has been my biggest breakthrough was learning to take responsibility for my choices and learning about the choices that I've made. I remember very early on when I started the business that I was very resentful, even to my wife? Which looking back at is just unbelievable. I was resentful because she was staying at home with the baby, while I was out in the "world of the unknown", basically responsible for "making it happen", when the reality is, is that is exactly what I chose. I had a big breakthrough early on within the first year, where I asked myself questions such as, what else would you rather be doing with your life? If I could do anything else with my life what would I be doing? Why am I bitching was the underline basis of these questions? I answered that I would be doing exactly what I was currently doing, and I felt a surge going through my body which was like, WOW, because I realized that I was bitching and complaining about living the life of my dreams. I had some serious self-talk because I knew that I had to man up, step up and to take care of this! This was a significant breakthrough and instantly one that changed my entire life. In the fore front my relationship, I was finally able to give my wife the appreciation, gratitude and love that she deserved. That has been a huge turning point in our level of communication with each other and in the strength of our relationship today. I am very grateful for that. It was something I didn't realize that was going to be part of the equation when I signed up for entrepreneurship when start your own business. It looks incredible from the outside and it's a different world from the inside, and I choose it every single day. Its just a matter of you don't know until you know. (the best way I can explain it) You don't know until you have been there and experienced it.

Then it is a matter of do you choose to stay here? or do you choose to do something else? That was the biggest challenge, taking ownership and full responsibility of the choice to do or not to do.

The way I overcame my biggest challenges I would say, bar none was through education and personal development. Taking the time to invest in myself, to learn about myself, discover what I truly want, learning how to give gratitude, learning how to problem solve, learning how to manage my emotions, these are things I have been keenly working on and I know and discover every day that I need more development in these areas which urges me to pursue education to a higher level every single day because I now understand the value of it. Education has enabled me to expand, it has allowed me to take on higher levels of pressure while maintaining my emotions and learning to keep my cool. I am not saying that I am perfect because I still have days that I break but at this point in my life and career I note down those points and I debrief them. I tell myself what went right with that situation? What did I like about how I handled it? What did I not like about how I handled it? How am I going to proceed moving forward next time? If I don't have that simple process, its in one ear and out the other. I may potentially end up acting the same way next time, *so its progress not perfection.* That's how I have overcome it. That's how I continue to overcome it in the challenges I face with my company and in my life today. Through education and personal growth, I find an area that I feel I'm lacking in, I feel I could be utilizing as a better strength, which I may discover through a fault or a failure occurring in my life and then I commit to a period where I then study that topic. Personal behavior was a big realm I went in to. Communication brings back a memory of a situation I had with a client, that I handled very poorly. She was speaking with my administrative team, my teams feedback was that she was treating them very poorly and speaking down to them. I immediately started barking at her, about how she was treating my team, not taking her concerns into my considerations. She told me that I was a horrible communicator, that I knew nothing about communication skills and she hung up on me. The sad truth about this was that she happened to be 100% right! (and I knew it). This encounter led me to Dale Carnegie's training which was all based on his book "How to Win Friends and Influence People" and how to stop worrying and start living, which is all about human communication. Finding and discovering that every single person wants to be loved and appreciated for exactly who they are. This sounds like such a rudimentary concept, but to be able to understand it and apply it into my life is what I have been able to do today due to that failure experience. Overcoming challenges, education, personal development and paying attention, to where you feel you desire to improve, can't be forced upon you, it needs to be something that you desire because then you are actual attached to the value that you will get from investing in that area.

Is it worth it? Every single day it is! There are days where it is much more challenging than other days but it all comes down to growth. The growth that I have gained in my own life and in my personal life in how I am able to take care of my family and be the example for others has been life changing for me. I love being able to help people with their struggles and too see them flourish. I feel that I am in a much better position to do that now as I have been feeding myself with tons of information, courses, education and books. I literally feel I have gained several doctorates since college because I have made a massive commitment in investing in myself. I feel that I have engaged in study so much more now than I ever did in my life before as I now see the true value of it. It has 100% been worth it, putting myself in the entrepreneurial position which has engaged me into education at a higher level because I saw the value that it was going to bring to my business. What I did not see was the value it brought to my life, in everyday engagements and in social situations. Being able to help my wife, being able to contribute to her dreams and set those up with her, being able to give her advice that I could use so that she can really carve her path of fulfilment has been huge for me. I see that with my sons as well not forcing them into anything but in taking the time to see what is valuable to them in their lives and being able to support that because they know I love them and I wouldn't want to change them, and I don't. I know I would not have that knowledge had I not delved into this, so I am 100% saying yes, it is worth it!

My dream life, I can honestly say that the life that I'm living today is my dream life. The reason I say that is because I realize, and I know for a fact, I am 100% certain that only I have control of the choices that I make every single day. I really think that what every single person desires Is the sense of control, that they are in charge of their own lives, that they are the writers of their own destiny. I truly feel that although right now, my life is full of challenges, I understand that a challenge is an opportunity. I am aware that I am probably going to fall several times, but I'm hell bent on learning and getting back up.

In these moments I know that I have the knowledge to approach it differently next time, so that I am propelling and pushing forward the next time that I encounter the same or a similar challenge in my life. Because of that sense of control, I feel free, yes there is stress, yes there is struggle, yet I feel free, because I feel I have the choice at all times, whether I desire to do something or not so I don't feel forced in my life, that's why I feel that this is my dream life!

Is it easy? It's as far from easy as it could possibly be. That's the perfect synchronicity of the situation. On the other side of the coin, there is no place id rather be, because I recognize the amount of growth its something that is an everyday occurrence, this never turns off. It's something I have learned to grow into, it's something I choose every single day. I choose every day to continue with this. I could choose to say I am done with this and that I am going to move on or, I am going to be an employee. I could just sit back. That's the part of the equation that scares me most, then it wouldn't be easy. I would feel locked in a box with a ceiling, sides and a bottom as well. That's it, there is growth potential in companies, but what the biggest hold back for me would be that I am not living my dream. I am not fulfilling my own visions, in that circumstance, so that's why I choose to stick with that difficult path, it's not easy and it's something that doesn't turn off.

Entrepreneurship is definitely not for everyone! When you finally grasp the concept of being able to do what you love and turn that into a service or product that not only does it inspire and empower you, but it also inspires and empowers others.

Then you know you have something extremely special! One of my foundational principles is reciprocity, which is taking all the knowledge you have acquired, applied it to your own life, have benefitted so so greatly from, then taking that knowledge and spreading it to as many other people as you possibly can, who you feel could benefit from it just like you have. This is what I get to do every single day. This is why I choose the difficult path, because of what it has given me in return, is such a higher level of love, appreciation and gratitude for what I get to do every single day. Now I'm not waking up saying "I have to do this, I need to this, I should do that..." I am living a life I truly get to say, "I get to do this, I chose to do this, I love doing this every single day", and that honors and humbles me, to the point where I give it as much gratitude and appreciation that I possibly can. I am not saying I am perfect and every single day is like that, but the majority of the time it really is. When it's not, my goal is to prove to myself why I want to be feeling gratitude and love for this? Why do I want to be feeling gratitude and love for the challenges I am going through right now? I ask myself a simple question, how does this challenge benefit me? How is it going to benefit me in the values that are most important to me in my life? As soon as I answer that, it then becomes apparent and that's exactly why I choose this life.

What drives me? My family. They inspire me, being around them gives me fulfilment, knowing that I am doing what I love, and that I have turned it into a vocation, I am able to support them through it. Every single day I am grateful for it. I will fight and out work anyone to keep it in my life. The second thing that drives me is doing what I love! Being able to do what I love gives me the constant gratitude to continue to push myself further and further to ensure that I am the best. I am very competitive in that sense because I want to be the best, not in the industry but the absolute best that I can possibly be and put out there so that I'm really representing my uniqueness through that. I get to do what I love so being authentic and being transparent in what I am doing has become more and more important to me through my growth and that drives me big time.

Next would be growth. I have a huge thing about always feeling like I'm improving. One of my mentors Pat Rigby told me either 'you're getting better or you're getting worse because there is no in between'. Every day I want to be able to say YES, I got better today, I achieved that growth. My personal philosophy is challenge, empower, and grow. We step into a challenge by stepping out into the unknown, stepping out of our comfort zone. Many times, in those situations we fall, in fact if we are stepping out far enough where will probably fall but once we do that we learn. That's the learning opportunity, once we grasp the point that failure is an opportunity then we run towards failure, because we learn it's an opportunity to say what went right? what went wrong? How am I going to improve moving forward? And this leads to empowerment, the second piece of my philosophy is when you become empowered you start to believe in yourself. You begin to have faith, you start to strategize, to plan and prepare, apply in your life, and that leads to growth. Challenge, empower and grow. I am obsessed with growth. Finally, I would say contribution, I want to be able to serve as many people as I possibly can. I feel blessed with what I have been able to receive, through education and in everything I have been able to learn and apply. Everything I have been able to learn from so many other people, through watching them. I want to be able to spread that to as many people as I can. I know that there is so much benefit and I want to see other people thrive. I love that! That's when reciprocity comes into play. Being able to give back to someone else, give them information or strategies, coaching that enables them to empower themselves so that they become inspired then they grow. Being able to see that is incredible. Contribution is a huge thing that drives me. I want to leave a footprint, a legacy, a contributing factor to where I feel I gave back to others and added value to their life. Period!

My why really comes down to growth, (I know I mentioned this before) it really is growth in all areas of my life. My highest values are:

1. **My family**
2. **Business development and research**, both those coupled together, both studying it and applying it.
3. **Exercise and nutrition,** both the learning and the application.
4. **Financial growth**, financial growth in terms of the more finance I have the more contribution I can do, the more ventures I can get involved with, the more people I can impact.

My why becomes growth, growth in all areas in my life, most specifically are those areas. Growth in my family, growth in my ability to grow my business and expand my knowledge base. Growth in my exercise and nutrition skillset, knowledge and application. Also, growth in my finance so I can continue to extend and contribute to a higher level. Naturally my why I want to get better, I want to challenge myself I want to grow from a spiritual sense, a sense of knowing, and from the sense of application and contribution.

I will leave you with this, the greatest discovery I have learned through my time as an entrepreneur is that every single person is the same, we all have desires we all have dreams that we want to make happen. The only difference between someone who makes it happen and someone who doesn't is, who is going to make the choice to do whatever it takes to earn the right to live the life exactly the way we wanted to. It all comes down to making the choice and doing the work. Many people have the perception that entrepreneurship is easy or that they could do it easily. Maybe it would be easy for them, maybe they could do it? I really see so many people talking talking talking, (I am guilty of this as well) we talk and we talk and we talk, and we don't act. Only massive action is going to help you acquire it, is it going to be scary? 100%. If it's not scary then you're not stepping out of your box enough. Those are words I tell myself every single day and that's the truth. We all have this choice every single day to do or not to do. The question is, are we going to do it through the thick not just the thin, doing whatever it takes to earn the right to live our life exactly the way that we want it to be. I am so humbled to be here, thank you so much for your time. If there is any way I can serve you, please do get in touch thanks again and enjoy the rest of your day.

Author of the books.

3 Minute Mindset

Fit Body + Fit Mind = Fit Life

Trevor Buccieri

Facebook.com/TBgrowthacademy

3

Relationships and Mindset

My name is Anna Garcia, founder of the Relationships Intensive Program for Women. Where did my journey start? Well, let's see. It started back in 2007 when I was a facilitator working for a company that helped the job centre get the unemployed back into employment. At the time, it started as a yearning, a deep, deep yearning to want to do more, to be more, to reach out more. There was a yearning to express who I really was in the world, I felt that working for somebody else didn't allow me to do that. It felt like having a ceiling over my head. As grateful as I was for my first job out of Uni, I felt stagnated after three years. I grew a lot within that company, but I felt stagnated I felt like there was so much more I was supposed to be doing. Luckily for me, that yearning was a lot more powerful than my fear. As scary as it was, it gave me the courage to just step out. I was 27 years old. I was living with a partner at the time who allowed me financial flexibility to leave work and start my business. I started it in a way that I wouldn't do that again. I left my job and then began my business. Today I would recommend if I were to do it all over again, I would make sure that I'd build up my business while I worked full time, so that I wasn't in scarcity. I spent a lot of time in scarcity, especially after six months into the business, I decided I could longer be in that relationship. I really faced scarcity. There were many times where I would face my screen looking at my bank account with tears going down my cheeks not knowing how I was going to pay rent that month. I wouldn't recommend that for anybody. That where my entrepreneurial journey began.

Today, I look back and I also don't regret it. I'm also very grateful because that was character building obviously. It was a massive lesson. My journey began when I began to receive. In my case, I received one or two opportunities. Because of my full-time job, I'd exposed myself a few times and I received a couple of opportunities. I ended up facilitating for the Greenwich Council in London for the unemployed, for mom's particularly. That's where the journey began.

I didn't know for a second how big it was going to get. Also, to kind of give you the duality I was in, although I was teaching people how to get back into work, there were many moments I remember delivering certain exercises or getting them to do bits and pieces in the workshop where I would be staring out the window going, "Oh my God, I feel unemployed myself," because it was contract work. It was varied. It was infrequent. I always felt like I was unemployed if I wasn't in the training room. I was just adapting to the entrepreneurial life. I was just adapting to the idea that I wasn't to be in the same place at the same time every day. That took time. Another thing, I wasn't surrounded by entrepreneurs, so I didn't know what was normal. I only had the programming of an employee, so it was a very painful process to do by myself. The biggest challenge was, indeed, the breaking out of an employee mentality, breaking out of the fears that came with the insecurity or the perceived insecurity that came with the entrepreneurial life. The greatest challenge was knowing what I needed to focus on. See, when you're employed, you can focus on systems and paperwork and pushing paper if you like and you still get paid. As an entrepreneur, you need to be client facing, you need to be on that phone, you need to be putting your value proposition in front of your client every single day. If not, you're dead. The biggest challenge for me was to learn that. I learned it in a very hard way over the years. I learned it the very hard way when I'd push paper for so long that I'd run out of funnel. I didn't have enough business to go around.

It took me years to understand, this was the biggest challenge. You must be in front of your client or calling your clients every single day. Business development is key every single day. It was adapting that mentality that is the business. I thought that my business was facilitation or that it was speaking. No. The business, whatever business you are in, your area business development company training or providing a training service rather or providing what service it is, but you are a business development company. This was the biggest challenge for me to get my head around. When I did, it exploded my business. It took a long time and it took guidance for me to finally understand that.

How did I overcome it mentor? 100% mentoring. It's not in our human nature to want to stay in the uncomfortable. What I got taught by my mentor was watching him being able to comfortably sit in the uncomfortable for long periods of time. That is the difference between an entrepreneur and a nonentrepreneur. A good entrepreneur is able to sit in the uncomfortable for extended periods of time. That's what I began to do. In my business today, my business development time is from 8:30 in the morning until 8:00 in the evening. I pretty much spend that whole time on the phone just calling client after client. That is very uncomfortable, especially when you're facing rejection all day long.

One of the biggest challenges, again, is going over or being able to be with rejection. We avoid rejection like the plague. How did I overcome it? Again, number one, having a mentor to say, "That's okay. You're supposed to live in the uncomfort. That's a whole reprogramming." I didn't realize. I was like, "Oh my goodness. What I need to do is be comfortable with the uncomfortable." That's number one. I needed to surround myself with people who were doing the same thing and listen to those conversations again and again. Secondly, be in action. There is only one way to get through the uncomfort. There is only one way to break through the fear of rejection and it is through being rejected. I wish there was an easier way, but it is the only way I have found. Being on the phone, always being in front of your clients, risking making a fool of yourself, risking being rejected, but that is the only way that I learned.

What is my dream life? This is my dream life. There is no other life. This is my dream life. I believe that when you get that, your life changes. My dream life is living by the river with my lover doing what I absolutely love. Today, I live by the river with my lover doing what I absolutely love. There are moments where I'm like, "No, no, no. Something else is my dream life." Then I remember, no, this is it. This is all there is. Can I get an upgrade version of it? Yeah. Would I rather live further up the river in more central London, yeah, why not? We can definitely do that, but in the meantime, I believe it's important that I live my dream life right now. This is my dream. Was it always like this? No, but I also believe it's a state of mind. I choose to see my life as I'm living the dream life right now.

Is there an extension to that dream life? As I say, upgraded living by the river, for sure. Expanding my business even more, for sure. Reaching out to more people, for sure. If there is a dream beyond this dream, it's just to reach out to even more people, to internationalize even more. It's just an expanded version of the right now to continue growing. That would be my dream life.

What is your dream life and is it easy? When I said your dream life is right now. When you make peace with right now, there is no other place to be. There is no place I'd rather be than sharing this information with you right now. The next minute ... In four minutes, I'm going to be in a phone call. There's no place I'd rather be. The moment I start thinking there is somewhere else I would rather be, then I'm not living my dream life right now.

Is it easy? It's brain training. It's training your mind that we are happy. We are happy who we are right now.

What drives you and what's your why? To be absolutely frank, the empowerment and transformation of human beings. I focus on the women because I believe women are CEOs of their families. When chief energy officers of their families, wherever they're at energetically impacts the rest of the family. What drives me is to see every woman that comes to me with terror going on in her life and in her mind, in her mind primarily, to be able to have her see that she can have peace instead. That drives me. My why, I would love to know that I go back to heaven and I know I honoured my Creator. I know like I know that I had a mission when I came on this planet and my why is to fulfil that mission every day, for me to go to bed every day with peace in my mind, with peace in my heart. That is my biggest why.

My next why would be my mother. Absolutely love being able to give her choices and provide better circumstances for her life and for her health. Then, it's my partner and I being able to continue to expand and have the choices that we've always wanted to have, to live how we want, where we live, how we want to live with the people that we want to do it with. My ultimate why is knowing that I came here, I showed up every day and that I fulfilled on the mission I came here to do or, at the very least, I died trying. There you go. That's me. Thank you.

If you're ready to transform your relationships and have the experience of a lifetime, you can register:

Anna Garcia

www.learn.relationshipsintensive.com/free-event

4

If I Can Do It So Can You

You do know that Every magical story starts with "Once upon a time". Even though it did not feel like that at times, spending long hours, lots of hard work, crazy frustrating thoughts and discouraging moments, it shaped out to be a fun journey and a story worth sharing.

Growing up I wasn't the brightest spark on the block academically, but with the encouragement and support of my family that they made me believe that it is possible to do anything I put my mind to. Saying that, I was unaware what I can do, because of my limiting beliefs, and how I can shape my own life into a magical story. All through high school, college and university I was very much into music. I Love to sing, play drums and spin records and just be around people. While in college one of the reasons I stayed there for seven years was because we had a band with my sister and two close friends that I loved performing with. I graduated with an associate degree in radio production and a BA in Liberal arts and communication. During that time, I was performing in clubs in the night life industry on my island of Cyprus, where my last fulltime occupation was as a food and beverage manager in restaurants and events halls, working extreme crazy long hours. As my position got higher, my free time was limited and so was my pay cheque. You did notice that my job was nowhere near to what I studied and showed interest in as the younger version of me. I constantly thought "was that it for me? I'm 35 and is this how I want my life to be"

Then one day, one of the two close friends that I previously mentioned, calls me up out of the blue and asked if I was free for a jam that night. It was a leaving party for a few university friends, we were to meet and have a small reunion and just play music like we used to for old times sakes. Even though I was ashamed to say it, I was rusty because the last seven years working on my career as a manager, creating someone else's dreams I did not even for five minutes play a musical instrument or even spin one single record. I agreed to go. It was my first night off in a very long time. As I got to the venue I was very excited to see everyone. I looked around and noticed there was no equipment set up. As you do we started with a few drinks that lead to a few more until one friend shouts out "let's do this" and they were all in on it, they all got up in the same direction, we all somehow started walking outside the venue in to the ally. A carpet comes out and randomly a few musical instruments started to show up. The idea was to go busking in the ally way to entertain people passing by. At this point I froze looked at my friend with a frustrated angry look saying, "dude what are we doing here?" he replies "Busking" I reply with a sarcastic tone saying, "I can see that". Backwards and forth in conversation I basically said, "I am a food and beverage manager of this place, how does it look if people see me doing this?" He then replies "wow, I've known you for many years and never thought I would see the day when Talal gave a bleep about what people thought of him?" WOW that was a huge thing to comprehend at the time. That was the first 'ah-ha' moment for me so I discreetly left and needed my own space to comprehend what was said. It did not take me long and I remember that I joined the group of jamming smiley faces. We played, sang and drank till the early hours of the morning. we raised 78 euros that night for more drinks of course. The next day I woke up more alive than I had ever been. Five days later, I quit my job.

I went back to my passion of playing music and started searching for income generating activities. Not a job. Everybody thought I was nuts to leave what I had worked for all these years. Until one day a close friend (who I look up to and call her and her brother my coach and am grateful for) introduced me to the concept of network marketing. For me that is where my true journey began. I got into personal development. Started meeting other coaches and mentors that were introducing me to books, different teachings, authors That opened a whole new world up for me. I love people. I love helping people. I love being part of a team and encouraging others. It really was something that I was doing anyway, as a professional in my work. encouraging people to be better at their jobs. But that was what it was. I inspired people to be better at a job, but I never realized that I can inspire people to work on themselves and not just their career.

That was another 'ah-ha' moment for me.

Things were not easy at first. I had doubts, that inner voice telling me what I can and can't do. Secondly, I had my closest friends, the dream stealers telling me their opinions about everything. Thirdly, I never knew what my gift was.

I never realized what I had inside me. I always put myself down. I was always trying to please other and I was always trying to be part of the crowd, instead of being the crowd. The more I read and attended seminars and pushed myself to become the best version of myself and what God intended for me, I was not walking on that path. Whatever I was learning was not in alignment with what I believed at the time, because It wasn't in alignment with my thoughts, and I wasn't in alignment to my goals. I had to change my focus, I had to change the language I was using. It all started with how I spoke to myself. How I showed up at meetings. If I was thinking something and it is a negative thought I started doing the opposite.

Then one day I heard this phrase "whatever's meant to be is up to me". I started walking on a different path. People will always have their opinions about me anyway, so I don't care if I please them or not, as long as what I'm doing is in alignment with what I want for my life, family and by grace of God I started to make drastic changes.

I started seeing this affecting other, gratitude from simple things that started happening in all our lives. Having More Fun as I started meeting more powerful and enthusiastic people. One mind set and a common goal. Helping others achieve personal goals. Changed the way I thought, for example instead of making money from people, I learned, how to make money with people. And to celebrate everything along the way. That was a huge boost and learning curve as our team began to grow. It gave me satisfaction to give back and share, especially when in a career, it was a dog eat dog world that I had been used to. As long as what I'm doing is in alignment with where my life balance is. If something felt great in your heart, then just go for it. Regardless of what people think about it. Best advice I can give is. Keep trying. Keep going for it, that idea you might have today, something might hold you back because of some reason or another, somebody else later down the line might think of the same thing and will have success with it because they took it and made it into an opportunity. Create good habits and celebrate them daily not just the results. Do things based on loving what you do and not from fearing if you will do it. It's in moments of decision that my fate changed. I was scared to leave my career behind. But it felt good in my heart it made me happy and it brought me joy as it became a new adventure, then pass that gift forward so you can help others along the way and in the end, you will find that, that is success. For someone to live a good life, it's all based on what's around you. Having fun while you're doing it. Are you able to travel and experience cultures not just to watch them on tv? As I started sharing, every story has THE END but not this one. I am just getting started on my journey. In my eyes, that is success for me. It's being able to do what I love and love what I do, and just help people while you're doing it. Put your family and others first with everything that you do. My analogy for family is Fulfil All Moments in Life Yesterday, as what I do today will shape what I want to become tomorrow. Never hold back on things and especially when it comes to your goals. If I can do it so can you.

Talal Sany Kawar

Facebook.com/talal.tbone

Talalstory Snapchat & Instagram

"The best way to find yourself is to lose yourself in the service of others."

-Mahatma Gandhi

5

A Quest for Inner & Outer Success

Who am I? Why am I here? What's my purpose? What is the meaning of my life? These are the questions I ask myself every day. To find purpose and meaning during my lifetime is my ultimate quest. On the surface, we can generally answer the "Who" question because it's simple. We most often view our identities as our names, our gender, our ethnicity, or our jobs. Another way to answer is where we come from, what we have experienced, our trials, our hardships, our obstacles, and how we have overcome adversity. The 'who question' is the very essence of who we believe we are. So, when I question myself as to who I am, my most honest response is to say I am an advocate, a fighter, a hunter, a force, a man, and a student.

I am an advocate and a fighter. I fight for social justice - the belief that everyone has the right to equal opportunity and access to benefits within society. These include equal opportunity in education, employment, business, healthcare, justice and legal representation, and much more. In short, I believe everyone is entitled to fair and equal treatment because of their inalienable right to equality designated in the United Nation's Universal Declaration of Human Rights and the United States Constitution. No human being should be 'less than' or 'separate' because of their class, ethnicity, gender, race, religion, economic status, education level, age, mental health status, criminal background, or any other classification. I fight for these rights of equality because I believe it is my duty. When I see people being taken advantage of, it bothers me deep in my core. I feel it in my whole body as my heart begins to beat faster, my chest gets tight, and I can't help but stand up and speak. There have been moments that I have thought of staying silent, but I can't seem to keep my voice from speaking.

I wasn't always that way. It took me time and experience to find my voice. For a long time, I was comfortable in silence, comfortable in ignorance and denial. It was easy to look the other way and pretend oppression didn't exist and inequality wasn't real. The mind is a powerful thing, which we have the power to open or close. We are always making choices, both consciously and unconsciously, as to what we see and what we choose to know at any given moment in time. We can only know and see what we know and see. The rest is what we have yet to learn.

My name is Orion and I was named after the constellation in the sky. Within the constellation of Orion is the Orion Nebula, where one can see the birth of stars even without a telescope.

Imagine - the birth of stars! That's wild! In Greek and Roman mythology, Orion is the Hunter and son of Poseidon, the God of the Sea. What does it mean to be named after a son of a God?

I don't take it in a literal sense. Instead, my parents found it to be a magical name and my father found the constellation to be his favourite.

How do I see myself as a hunter? I believe that I am always learning and through that I must continuously seek and 'hunt' for information, things I don't know. After all, I don't know what I don't know. How can I know what I don't know? The only way I can is to seek. To do this I must read, watch, speak, learn, discuss, ask, question, and make lots of mistakes. To hunt is to always be looking for answers. I consider this to be one of my greatest qualities. To be alive in a world full of information and have the privilege to access the internet to see, hear, read, and watch people write, teach, and preach their message across multiple platforms is the great miracle of today. My duty as a student of life is to hunt for answers, to learn as much as I can, to know more, so I can learn more about who I am, why I am here, what my purpose is, and ultimately to find meaning.

In 2016, I was working in an excellent and stable job in sales, I thought I had a great career. I was married, had a nice car, a nice house, and all the outside things that I thought I needed to be successful. I thought, "Why don't I feel successful? I have everything as a result of my hard work, but why do I feel like my life could be better? Why do I feel unfulfilled?"

I started asking deeper questions such as "What is success? How do I define Success? Do I want to be rich? Do I want to be happy? What do I want? What am I missing?" These questions required an inward look at my motives: why was I working in the occupation I chose and why was I in the marriage I was in? Everything was related to everything else. Did I create a world for myself because I wanted the results so badly? In other words, did I think that if I created all the outside symbols of success, I would achieve success inside? The answer is, I never felt successful inside because I was chasing the wrong goals. I didn't see that at first, it took a while to see why I felt lost mentally, emotionally, and spiritually.

How does one feel satisfied? Where does that feeling come from? Does it come from pleasure, pain, overcoming challenges, meeting goals, or walking through fears? For me, it came through forgiveness. It took me awhile to find the source and forgive. Once I did, I found freedom from all the feelings that kept me locked up, kept my mind imprisoned, kept me limited and stuck. The part of my mind that held me back says to me that my ideas are worthless and that nobody cares. Once I was able to forgive, I was able to love and, subsequently, let love into my heart. Once I was able to let love into my heart, I was able to love others. Now, that I can love others, I can choose to replace my fears with love.

The man who taught me to forgive was also the man who taught me to be silent. When I was 20 years old, in 2006, a detective called me from the San Mateo police department asking if I would tell my story in a deposition. It was a case against a prominent child psychiatrist in northern California. The authorities had seized all his medical files and they had come across my name and file. At this point, the officer had said they had reached out to hundreds of patients and no one was willing to come forward. He also said that if I agree to give my deposition that I would also need to agree to testify, and my story would be out it the open forever. Because of the internet my name would always be associated with the psychiatrist's and with this case. It was a risk, since we didn't know if we would win or lose the trial. I needed a couple days to think it over.

The next three days I thought about everything. The same memory that had been playing in my mind every day of my life of that man was a nightmare that I tried so hard to forget. Now, it was going to be made real for the whole world to see. I isolated so much of my life to protect myself from forming relationships because of the confusing relationship I had with this man. Was I ready for the world to know about it? My silence was clearly about survival for me. Now, everything changed. Was I surviving? Was I thriving? Or, was I haunted by my memories and haunted by my fears? What if people knew the truth, what would they think of me? All these questions flooded my thoughts, totally consuming me. Then I thought to myself, "How do

I stop him? How do I stop his behaviours? Perhaps even more importantly, how can I protect others from this man's monstrous, predatory behaviour? What can I do to protect children from a psychiatrist who is sexually abusing his patients? What can I do in my power to change these circumstances?"

The answer was to testify and tell my story. Why? To protect others, to say "NO," to publicly name his behaviour, and to finally voice that I did not give him permission because I was just a child.

A week later I flew up to the San Mateo Police Department in northern California to give my deposition and was accompanied by my sister who served as my legal counsel. A couple of months later I found out that other victims came forward because of my testimony. In 2009, we went to trial.

Even though I was silent for eleven years, I also found my voice through that experience. It was one of the hardest obstacles I have ever had to overcome. It took challenging work, a lot of therapy, and a lot of 'blood, sweat and tears.' It required me to look at my motives, my behaviours, my actions, my thoughts, my feelings, and my intentions. The years of work on myself was necessary if I was to overcome the bondage I experienced because of the silence. It was necessary for me to speak up, to find confidence in myself, to risk everything for something bigger than myself. It was never about my reputation, or about what everyone will always know about me. It was always about justice.

When I was on the stand at the trial the defence asked me why I wasn't pursuing the defendant in civil court for damages (financially). I responded, "This is not about money, it never was. I don't want his money." The defence thought I was financially motivated to give my testimony, but that was never the case. I gave my testimony because what he did over many years to so many was wrong, plain and simple.

I am an advocate above all else. Ever since the day I gave my deposition and chose to speak openly to the press, I have felt this call to stand for those seeking justice. Where I see people in positions of power taking advantage of those without power, I cannot help but speak out and advocate for equality.

In 2009, the first trial ended in a hung jury, a mistrial, and I didn't understand why we lost. I was angry for a long time, I didn't know how to forgive because I didn't want to forgive. Anger kept me from letting love into my heart. It also kept me from seeing the truth. Anger kept me in ignorance and denial, it allowed me to see what I wanted to see, not what I needed to see. Anger gave me permission to hate, permission to be justified in actions that were not in alignment with how I wanted to live my life.

I felt as if the world and everything else was going against everything I wanted in life. I found out later that it was my inner, unhealed projections that filtered my perceptions of my life and it had nothing to do with the world. The more I was angry, the more I attracted negativity in my life. I could not receive positive energy because I was always focused on the hate. I could not receive love because I was so focused on resentment. I was selfish and self-seeking. I didn't want to learn new things because I thought I knew enough.

When I think back to the most difficult challenges of my life, they are challenges that have limited the way I think and perceive the world. Every limitation I have imposed on myself is caused by an experience I have lived, which is rooted in a fear, which can be traced back to a reason why I am trying to protect myself out of survival. The story of the psychiatrist is a perfect example because it has to do with trauma that spans relationships, intimacy, trust, self-esteem, resilience, beliefs, and my own values for myself over many years. Every one of our experiences affects us. We all respond in different ways. In my case, I immediately tried to avoid having close relationships with others or letting myself become vulnerable with others, including my family for many years. This limited my reality and what I allowed myself to believe about what was true, what could be true, and what was possible.

On August 7th, 2013 I had the opportunity to face Dr. William Ayres and tell him directly that he didn't have power over me anymore. I was able to forgive him for what he did and move forward with my life. That same day, he was sentenced to 8 years in federal prison.

Why is this important? For me, I needed to forgive him and forgive myself for the anger I held onto, forgive myself for the relationship we built together, for the feelings I felt with him, and for feelings of shame, guilt, and anger. I needed to both forgive myself and him for the whole thing. Forgiving him was the hardest thing I have ever done. I remember my close friend telling me I had to forgive him, if I was going to find peace. I said, "You're crazy! I'll never do that." But, forgiveness does not mean that we forget, or that we condone bad behaviour in any form. It just means that if we want to let ourselves out of the prison of pain and condemnation, then we forgive.

Forgiveness is also a process. It wasn't just done in one day and that was it. It takes many days, weeks, months and years. I still forgive him every day. It's a practice for me. I have to remember that he made mistakes, just like I have made mistakes. He deserves just as much love as I deserve. I want the best for him and I pray for him. That is how I found peace in my heart.

Getting right in my mind is important because I cannot be right in my business life if I am not right in my personal life or my heart. When I think about what my purpose is, why I'm on this Earth, what the meaning of my life is, I think about my experiences. When we choose to understand and learn from our experiences, it makes us more qualified to speak about our truth. I know for a fact that I'm here to be an advocate due to the experiences I've gone through in my life. It is clear to me that I'm here to fight for social justice. That journey began for me as young as nine years of age. I didn't know it yet, but I realized it when I was twenty and finally decided to speak my truth.

I've always loved helping others in my spare time, through nonprofit volunteering, raising money for causes I care about, or mentoring youths. Why do I do those things? Because I love serving others, I love helping them. It's not about me, it never is, although I do know that in helping others, I heal myself. How can I support them in finding their purpose, their calling, their mission? I'm all about asking questions, thought provoking questions that I think we need to be asking as a collective species. I'm doing that with those I work with, both online and in person, in a free interchange. It doesn't require me to charge money to ask a question and it doesn't require us to exchange funds to have a conversation. After all, you do all the hard work of answering the hard questions for yourself and you receive the rewards. All the greatest thinkers and philosophers historically have asked questions and that's all I'm doing, asking questions. In doing so, I hope I am helping you find your answers as I have found the answers to them for me. Your answers will most likely be different. The important piece is that we seek, continue to seek, and never stop seeking. We can keep expanding our minds by asking new questions; always reading the opinions and experiences of others; and learning and gaining knowledge from the experiences of friends, family, and mentors/teachers whom we respect and admire.

When I ask you questions like ...

Why are you here on this Earth? What is your Purpose? What is your Mission?" to charge you for answers, I of course know that nobody has *the* answer to those questions. They are all dependent on the individual and the discovery of the answer for each person. So, how do we channel these answers and ideas into a business? That's where my entrepreneur journey began.

While I was in college I started selling ads for the school newspaper, because I loved doing it. Sales was a game for me and I loved playing it. The school ended up giving me a Journalism scholarship for my efforts. I went on to graduate *Cum Laude* from Hawaii Pacific University with a Bachelor of Science in Advertising/Public Relations with a focus on Strategic Communication. I went into sales and marketing for a career since I was good at it. It seemed like a wise idea at the time. Sales came easily to me, as did customer service, marketing and branding. I was hired right out of college and I started working for Enterprise Rental Cars.

They started me at $36,000/year with benefits. I worked my way up to Management Assistant and I was offered a job in walking distance from my house. It was the job I thought I wanted. Then I received a call from my father who needed help running one of his businesses. He needed someone with a sales background to take over and revamp his brand. At this time, I was starting my own life in Hawaii and beginning my own professional story. Meanwhile, my father needed help. So, my wife and I decided to move to Santa Barbara to assist him with his business, because family comes first. In exchange for returning home the arrangement for financial compensation was rent and $36,000/year, but no benefits. I thought it was only fair to charge a little more for the experience I had gained over the past year, but I wasn't making money hand over fist. I stayed at the company for one year in the Brand Manager position, before earning a promotion to Director of Sales, when I negotiated a commission structure.

If you have ever worked for family, it's no easy feat. For some, it can be done, but for me it was difficult. I had worked with my father before in high school when we had a restaurant, but I had never worked for him in the corporate sense. Growing up he was always the boss, and now as I was grown up, and in this position, he was still the boss. I couldn't escape or separate the two, while at work. It's hard to explain. Anyhow, I stayed at the company another year in the Director of Sales position to lift up the sales, launch on Amazon, and build out the social platforms. It was a small company, less than twenty employees. I had to remember that I was there to help my family. I never moved back for the money. However, I frequently found myself unhappy in my job, in my marriage and in my life overall. I didn't know why I was depressed all the time.

In December of 2014, when we first moved back to Santa Barbara, I started volunteering at a juvenile rehabilitation camp for male youth offenders. I went up to the camp once or twice a month for an hour or two. I would speak with the boys about their experiences, my experience, our shared experiences, and how we can all find purpose and value in those experiences, if we so choose.

It started with honesty and sharing from the heart and it grew from there. I loved going up there. I went every other week, once a month, or every week, as it varied depending on my schedule. Either way, I would always get up there, and I would love every minute of it. I could relate to them. We were similar, even though our circumstances were different, we found ways we could bond.

Every day, Monday through Friday I would go to work, handle my business, and the days I drive up to camp would vary. Sometimes it would be Wednesday, sometimes

Tuesdays, and sometimes Sundays. Whichever day it was, I looked forward to it. I think what I experienced there was unconditional love.

These kids accepted me for what I was too, just like I accepted them. For the times we were together, the walls of the camp disappeared. We laughed, shared stories, and read from books. They taught me to love unconditionally, they taught me to believe in myself, to trust myself, to honour myself, to respect myself. I both gave to them and received back in turn, reinforcing my belief that giving and receiving are connected.

On my 30th birthday my wife and I decided to part ways and get a divorce. It was mutual, and we agreed it wasn't working out. I was upset over it. I talked about it with the boys up at the camp and told them the truth, didn't sugar coat it, and they accepted me and my experience. They understood that things happen. They supported me, loved me, and showed up for me even when I was down. They changed my life.

Meanwhile, I was still working at my 9-5 job, separating from my wife, but I had found a passion that had lit something inside of me. I was lost for so long, but suddenly, I was motivated to find a way to help these kids find purpose and meaning in life after they were released. I started looking into ways to reduce recidivism and asking friends about their experiences. I had friends who were locked in prison for over thirty years and I wanted to know how they rebuilt their lives. What could I do that was in my power to help these kids? Then someone said to me in some words that I hear all too often. "You can't do anything to help those kids. They are stuck inside that situation.

Nothing you do can change their situation. It's a waste of time." I'll never forget those words. Those are the words of a person who is tired and who has given up. When I heard those words, I refused to believe them, because I know that anyone can change their life if they know that they can, and if they want to.

I'm proof of that. Anyone can change the course of their life if they earnestly want to, if they are given the right support, and if they work their asses off to do so. It takes a lot of work and you cannot give up, no matter how many times you hear words like that.

I knew in that moment something had to be done. I knew I was in the wrong job. I wanted to do something for these kids and I knew I first needed to build a non-profit. I always wanted to do that, but I didn't know where to start. I had attended a conference about nine months prior about creating your dream life. It was called the *Dream*Builder® LIVE Workshop with Mary Morrissey.

Essentially, I went there to build my dream life and I did. I imagined building a non-profit for kids and juvenile youth, similar to a retreat centre. I coloured in all the details, where it was located, how many would work there, what programs we would offer, how we would pay for everything. I created a plan for my dream. Then I came home and forgot all about it.

Nine months later I started thinking about it again. I called up my friend that I had met at the workshop. I asked her how she was doing on her dream. She said she was manifesting things well and things were on track. Then she asked me about mine, I responded "I haven't done anything. I don't know what to do or where to start." She said, "The best thing about us is that we can create whatever we want. We can build the life that we want to live. You can create that for yourself right now! You had mentioned that you wanted to go back to grad school in the past.

Have you investigated that?" I thought to myself, "She's right, I can do anything I put my mind to." For some reason everything clicked for me. I understood in that moment that she was right. I didn't have to be depressed if I didn't want to be. I didn't have to be sad for myself or feel sorry for myself, because I can choose to do something about it to change it! I replied,

"Yeah, I was looking at applying to USC and another school, the deadline is in a couple months. You're right! I'm going to apply. What the hell? If I get in, I guess this is where I'm supposed to be. I'll find out and let you know." I was accepted in August of 2016, just three months later, and started my classes immediately. I gave my notice at work and I started the next chapter of my journey.

As a student at the University of Southern California's Suzanne Dworak-Peck's School of Social Work, I have found my community. I am among people from all walks of life who are dramatically different in experience and time on this Earth. Together, we share a common goal. We all work to tackle the Twelve Grand Challenges of Social Work. We do these one at a time. The one I am focusing on is to Achieve Equal Opportunity and Justice. Each grand challenge is separate, but they are all focused on one common goal: to advocate for social justice for all. I am among many professionals who also desire both inner and outer success for others, and who support others in their pursuit of happiness and wholeness, because they deserve it. This is the community of which I have always wanted to be a part. I found it when I went looking, but I had to look, and to seek. I would have missed it if I didn't know what I wanted. We find what we want when we believe in ourselves.

Our hearts tell us what we want. It is our minds that distract us.

I'm now 32 years old and have discovered my purpose for this time in my life. I have found my passion, I know why I'm here, I know more of who I am, I know why I have been through my hardest experiences, and I know what I want to give the world.

At 30 years of age my purpose was to build a non-profit. So, I left my sales position and applied to graduate school because I didn't know how to build a non-profit. Today, I have launched my non-profit, the Social Justice Team (SJT). The most important lesson I've learned since switching careers has been that following my heart has been my greatest asset. It has led me to my purpose. Tapping into the heart, the passion, is authentic. In my experience, heart happiness often comes when we allow ourselves to be vulnerable enough to make a connection with another. Feeding my heart with the passion to serve others has led me to the birth of SJT. The Mission of the SJT is to provide free therapy and diverse supportive services to underserved populations in Los Angeles. My goal is to build a community where individuals can forget about the troubles of yesterday, today, and tomorrow, and instead focus on things that give them joy. To assist clients in discovering what they are passionate about, SJT will offer free counselling and group sessions to assist clients in looking inward, and introduce classes in health, exercise, meditation, mindfulness, music and art to give individuals an outward and alternative outlet. Through providing these services it is my hope that people will discover joy, happiness, and maybe a passion of their own.

Once I launched SJT, I met my initial purpose and I already had a new one. I didn't even have to brainstorm it. My new purpose is to make mental healthcare services accessible to as many people as possible at no charge. Now, the first step is through SJT and proving the model is effective with our organization.

No small task indeed!

When I think about my passion, it has never wavered, I have always loved helping others. It has been my favourite thing to do in my spare time, since if I can remember. So, purpose can shift, evolve, and change, but passions often stay the same. When nurtured our passions are bricks we build on every time we practice living them.

To know why I am here, I had to test different thought systems and occupations. I had to test things, taste them, feel them, touch them, see them. I had to experience life and get out of my comfort zone to know myself and know what I believe and don't believe and what I like and don't like. To know why I'm here I had to define my purpose and my passion, but also discover what I did not want. It's all a journey. We don't know everything in a matter of days, weeks, or months. It takes years and a lot of mistakes. However, sometimes the answers come quickly. For example, if we know our passions we can skip some time. For me, the more I serve others, volunteer my time, give myself to unconditional service, the quicker I find the answers I seek. It's up to each of us! That's what is exciting about our quest as individuals, to answer these questions.

To live one's dream life takes boldness, courage, bravery, consistency, focus, empathy, compassion, kindness, determination, tolerance, love, respect, integrity, faith, forgiveness, and acceptance, among other things. It is far from easy. My path is wide and there are lots of people on it who have my back, who are supporting me, but I'm alone for the most part and that's alright. I've found peace and independence in being alone on my quest. As an entrepreneur, I wear a lot of hats. Similar to everyone else, I'm busy.

The road to success is different for everyone. I define success as an inward journey of fulfilment often expressed outwardly. I believe I was successful when I quit my job and pursued my passion to serve others and build a non-profit. I believe I was successful when I took that leap of faith and believed in all my abilities to make it in this world. Success is a concept I choose to frame as a feeling inside my heart where I have overcome the odds and persisted. Failure is part of it too. It's just a mistake on the path of life, where I get up and try another way. It has been said that there are no failures in life, only successes that have not yet happened. This way of looking at the world takes the power out of the word failure, so I can focus on my successes.

The best advice I can give the new entrepreneur is to have the courage to set goals that to others might seem impossible, to trust your heart, and to follow your passion. A powerful way to find your purpose is to lose yourself in the service of others. At SJT, we are inspired by a quote from Mahatma Gandhi, "The best way to find yourself is to lose yourself in the service of others." Gandhi showed me how to find my purpose. If I remember that service to others is more important than serving myself, I will find direction in my life. At SJT, volunteering is a core aspect of how we assist individuals in Los Angeles. So, if you are starting out, remember that your purpose can change and evolve. Your passion might be more constant, so follow it and it won't steer you wrong. Your heart will lead you to happiness so trust it, follow it, have faith, and believe in yourself. Your abilities, your mind, and your heart, have infinite possibilities.

Orion Brutoco

www.socialjusticeteam.org

"The best way to find yourself is to lose yourself in the service of others."
-Mahatma Gandhi

6

Misunderstood to Reconnecting the World

I've always tried to find jobs where I could add a lot of value, one, but two, find something that I'm passionate about that didn't want to make it feel like it was a job. I think J-O-B is ... Job is a dirty word. Work should be fulfilling; it should be nice, it should be enjoyable. The industry that I moved into, I made an intentional decision to get into my industry, which is translation services because I love synchronizing people and businesses everywhere. I love different cultures. I love different languages. I love different people. I'm very, very open-minded, I've been in this industry 11 years. I launched my company seven years ago.

The job was okay. The management that I was working with didn't fulfil on a lot of their promises, and things just didn't go the way that they had said, or that I had wanted, and so we parted ways and then that's when I decided to start my own entity. But It wasn't too bad, I'd decided early on to get into a field that I just wasn't working to make money, I wanted to get into a field that I was interested in, that moved me down the path of creating my own business.

I studied finance through my bachelor's degree in undergraduate school, and I studied Information Systems through graduate school for my master's degree, and I wanted to synchronize business and technology. I saw so many opportunities; things weren't going the way that I had anticipated, hoped, as I was planning at the company I was currently. So, the breaking point was just a question I asked myself where I said, a question came up. The breaking point for me was when I asked myself the question, "When I'm 60 or 65 years-old, how am I going to feel about not chasing my dreams? How am I going to feel about not trying to build something that my heart and soul are pulling me to? How I'm going to feel about it? ... Am I going to regret it? That I'm going to wish that I had done it?" ... And I didn't want to leave like that. I said, "Come on, chase that dream. I'm going to do whatever I want," and that was the decision I knew right then, that hey I had to try to build my enterprise. Had to build my own company. I had to take the leap of trying to figure it out.

The company name is InWhatLanguage. We are a translation technology company with a social impact or a social impact that's core is its business. We work very closely with refugees in America to help integrate them into the communities through language support, language services, and English language learning at school. We also work very closely with U.N agencies and N.G.O's around the world. Like disaster-affected communities. So, communicating when there is a disease outbreak or a hurricane or a tsunami, where communicating is as important as food, water, and shelter. And we also work, of course on the private sector and the government side just to make translation faster, easier, and scalable.

So, our model is like Uber in that we have thousands of people around the world that login into our system, and they can capture content that comes in. It could be audio or video. It could be websites, documents, software. It's loaded on-demand, real-time and the people that work on my language and then by subject matters, they can grab the content that's available, localize it, adapt it, and push it back into the environment and the platforms and technology for our clients. So, like Uber for translations.

We work in over 200 languages. We have a presence in over 120 countries. And it's a growing model for a real shrinking world, a world truly becoming small and connected.

Well, there were challenges. When I started-up at the beginning, I think it was just overcoming fear first of all. And then just learning to see the beauty in the fears, seeing the beauty in the challenge, seeing the gift in all the learning and understanding that as I'm trying to do these things I will fall, and I will make mistakes. I was so hard on myself, but then I remembered that all my mentors say that overcoming challenges is the beauty of becoming an entrepreneur and running your own venture. It's not necessarily chasing the money. Although the money is great, and it helps with freedom and things like that, but it's the ability as a human being to feel a fulfilment and to know that you're growing and that you're progressing.

When you're at a job you're doing the same thing over and over, and over. It's just this cycle, and there is not a lot of fulfilment there. When you're an entrepreneur you're chasing your dreams and every day is different and every day is about growth and learning. I think that the biggest challenge earlier on was that I wasn't really embracing the learning process. I wasn't grabbing it and saying, "Hey, things are always going to be chaotic, there is always going to be challenges, but that's the beauty of it all just because that's when you really grow." You truly grow during tough times. Earlier on it was tough just to build up the brand, build up the technology, build up the teams, get the capital, get the clients, and monetize things, get some recurring revenue in, but I just made a commitment to work hard every single day.

I got very strategic about who I was spending my time with or wasn't. Where I was aligning myself with my social currency. Who I was talking to help me. Finding multiple mentors and models that work, that was successful and never stopping that, even now. We're seven years in, we're growing rapidly, and I still churn the same process of finding people that have done it better. Walk the path better and help me minimize my problems. Now it feels like I'm in a marathon and the gun just barely went off, and I'm in mile one of the marathon with another 25 miles to go. Because I've reinvented the vision. I've reinvented the company to look at our real potential now and say, "Wow, we really can become a global force of good. We can become a global brand, a global name." And not willing to be satisfied with just reaching, you know, a certain revenue level and trying to sell or, you know, my purpose is to help as many people as we can around the world to unify communities to use language and technology to pass information.

So, we can either lives or save lives. And that's scalable. It's very scalable. So, it doesn't stop. So, you know, where I'm at now, is just very excited about we secured a few million dollars in capital to grow faster, accelerate it.

And so, I'm looking forward to continuing to recruit, bring along the best people, bring the best people in business, in the company that makes all the difference to helping us grow and then continuing to chase the vision. I see a very, very big vision. You know that wasn't the case three or four years ago, so it's evolved as I continue to nurture that germ, so now I'm really looking forward to it and along the way helping as many people as I can, entrepreneurs and other people try to chase their dreams.

Our mission is to unify people and communities through innovative translation solutions.

We develop technology and human networks which enable knowledge and information to flow seamlessly between diverse communities, fostering trust and mutual understanding, increasing access to critical information, and improving lives.

Translation and access to information are critical forms of aid, which improve lives and strengthen communities around the globe.

With the support of our partners and language professionals, we provide free–or highly discounted– translation services to help meet the language and communication needs of vulnerable communities.

Cody Broderick
inwhatlanguage.com
Email: Codyb@.inwhatlanguage.com

"Come on, chase that dream, you owe it to your family, you owe it to yourself."

7

Impact and Influence

Brought up in a dysfunctional family with domestic violence, I suffered horrendous low self-esteem; I didn't trust my own opinion, I was reluctant to take on challenges, I accentuated the negative; I couldn't accept compliments at all, I neglected myself and used to take many different slimming pills to lose weight whilst working out in the gym as a gymaholic. I was obsessed with my weight as it was the only thing I had control over albeit superficially. I thought I was a person of zero value and had barely any boundaries. I also suffered from anxiety and emotional turmoil especially when I experienced rejection, lacking self-confidence and experiencing depression. I had an inability to be fair to myself, exaggerated concern over what I imagined other people were thinking, neglected myself, treated myself badly but not other people, worried tremendously whether I had treated others badly and then continuously apologised profusely. I also thought I was ugly and always compared myself to my friends and other people, feeling even more inadequate and useless. I was argumentative, following in my father's footstep because he used to argue and fall out with many people. I led an independent life with no emotional or mental support from my family. In my early teens, I used to sit in the bathroom holding a razor against my wrist but never having the guts to do it (thank God). However, when I was 17 and again when I was 21, I decided to take an overdose.

But what triggered all of this? It all began when my dad used to hit my mum and verbally abuse her; because he never loved my mum simply because she was not a white-skinned Asian woman nor a white-skinned European woman. This deeply enraged me. There was zero unity and zero support in our family and even though I grew up with three brothers, none of us were close. I was never spoilt as the only girl let alone protected. This is why I have always been able to speak up against injustices whether I am liked or disliked for it.

I lived away from home for seven years. I moved back home and realised that living in a volatile environment was not healthy for me; I was angry and agitated a lot of the time as well as depressed. I recognized that my career in corporate communications was not my calling in life and I felt deeply unhappy because I wasn't serving my purpose. What I was doing wasn't in line with my values, when all I deeply wanted was to make a massive contribution and difference in the lives of other people and leave a legacy behind. Where I went wrong - I realized I lacked confidence, rather than relying on myself and trusting my own judgment about what I enjoy doing, what I'm great at, what I should pursue. Instead I listened to other people. So, when I chose my degree I asked my eldest brother, who's nothing like me. I asked him, "Which degree shall I choose?" He said, "I would choose Management Studies because it's an all-round degree and it will help when applying for a job." I disliked Management Studies; I should have done something completely in line with my values and my interests instead. I did the same when I chose my post-graduate diploma.

Again, I studied a subject I yet again disliked: public relations. With funding from the NHS, I still went and did it anyway.

Despite my home environment, I had a relentless drive to study at university and some years after completing my BSc Hons degree in management studies, I completed a postgraduate diploma in public relations. This is because I was hard-wired to be independent! I worked across a number of jobs as a corporate communications professional (aka public relations) spanning the public, private and charity sectors including various NHS employers, Lambeth Council and King's College London. I remained unmarried and relied solely on myself to work hard and financially provide for me.

Eventually I moved out of the family home, as I'd hit my pain threshold; and boy did I have a seriously high pain threshold! I knew I couldn't take it anymore and that changing my environment was a necessity to my growth; it was nonnegotiable. When I moved out, I remember bringing my black bin liners downstairs and my brother pushing me out of the door. He said something horrible to the person that was helping me.

My career involved working with chief executives and senior managers, so I had to be confident. I had a lot of anger and resentment towards my mother and my father. I stopped talking to my dad when I was 16, after he'd threatened to kill us all. This was the final nail in the coffin for me, as it dawned on me that I hated this man who was my biological father. I stopped talking to him, which lasted most of the rest of his life. Then my dad contracted prostate cancer which later developed into full blown cancer. Towards the last few years of his life I did try to talk to him, but it was just insincere. I still hated him a lot because he disrespected my mum and used to hit my brothers. But I also had a lot of anger towards my mum because I believed she played the victim for the majority of her life and, despite my advice, she didn't seem interested in creating unity amongst her children. Now I wish I had been patient with my mum back then.

During my career, I was turned down for many jobs and rejected time and time again, but I never gave up. I even failed my driving test thirteen times and again I never quit; I persisted (and passed at the fourteenth attempt!). I couldn't understand why I kept failing and did whatever I could to make sure that I passed. I bought a cheap Vauxhall Corsa, I asked friends who were licensed drivers to sit with me and I changed my driving instructor four times. I even travelled all the way to Matlock in the Peak District and stayed alone in a bed and breakfast to attend a five-day crash course only for the instructor to tell me on day four that he couldn't put me through because he said that I wasn't ready. I returned to London and went straight to Guy's Hospital as my dad was admitted into intensive care.

I was also driven when it came to fitness. I was a serious gymaholic to the point where my friends would say: "Why don't you become a personal trainer? You practically live in the gym and have the body image to prove it." I did this for many, many years, working out consistently in the gym without fail and I would just go there alone. I was very driven. However, hardly no one knew that I popped slimming pills to keep my weight down as I was obsessed with my body image all because I felt worthless inside.

The real game changer for me was when I made the decision to attend Anthony Robbins Date with Destiny in Orlando and Landmark Forum education because I had enough of hating myself. I wanted to clear away the baggage and negativity weighing me down and holding me back. I wanted to explore and re-discover who I was. But I didn't stop there. I invested in many coaches to achieve long lasting personal transformation.

You see, whilst my childhood and adult life were difficult, overcoming these experiences have helped me to fall in love with the woman I am today and help many people to create the shifts and transformation to live an empowered life.

This brings me to my vision: the desire to travel internationally to transform and empower people regardless of creed, age, sex or background. This may also include entrepreneurs, corporate professionals, parents and children to achieve my vision to be of service to others, serving from the heart and giving endless value whether it's about health, wealth, relationships, spirituality, family, etc. It's all about result, results, results and I want nothing more than to work with my clients to achieve results. I don't deal with fluff. It's about decide, commit and succeed all the way. It's also paramount that I achieve this with integrity and authentically.

I am also creating a public-speaking platform because it is one of the most important yet most dreaded forms of communication but in the working and business world, and in personal relationships, public speaking is a vital skill to have and to hone. It effects simple, everyday interactions between co-workers, bosses and employees, professionals and clients, coaches and speakers, etc., and it can have an enormous impact on your career path, your level of success in your industry and in business and in your personal relationships with your children and spouse. So many coaches speak on stage, and wish to develop their confidence on stage, whether it's to sell or to create influence and achieve transformation in their audience' lives. Therefore, creating a public-speaking platform to help people become confident speakers is ideal because I get to the root cause behind their anxiety, lack of confidence and nervousness which can sometimes be low self-esteem, low selfworth, not feeling good enough or clever enough, or believing they are not as good as other people.

Due to the zero access to personal development as a child, I am also bringing personal development to schools and the youth.

Why have I mentioned youth? Because there are many issues affecting youth from substance misuse, cyber bullying, social media anxiety, inferiority complex, violence, depression and pressures to succumb to sex pressures and the inability to be able to talk to their parents without being judged. I want to empower youth to consider healthier alternatives to live an empowered life.

If you are ready to start your journey to transformation, come and join me and allow me to help you to unleash your leadership.

I offer one-to-one and group coaching on peak performance/life-coaching. I also deliver confidence-building workshops to help you to re-build or increase self-confidence as well as to achieve confidence in public speaking in business, the corporate sector or your personal life.

I am running a one-to-one 7-week Confidence Coaching programme and a 7-day confidence accelerator programme. Together, we look at your road map and re-define your blueprint, use NLP techniques, work through your core beliefs and values, achieve total clarity and mental toughness, master self-leadership, learn how to remain target focused and embrace setbacks to achieve peak performance in any area of your life.

Coaching people to become the best version of themselves from a place of integrity is an honourable and humbling experience. I want people to recognise that everyone's a leader; it's got nothing to do with job titles or qualifications.

> "You are good enough just the way you are, what can you offer right now"

Certified coach and certified NLP practitioner who is also passionate about mental health

Farah Butt

Facebook.com/FarahButt

Instagram: farahbuttofficial

Email: 44farahbutt@gmail.com
www.farahbuttcoaching.com

8

Queen of self-love helping you to tap into your inner peace.

I really want to share some of my story with you to let you know why I do what I do and the reason why I am able to help others. This is because of something that is deeply connected to me. Something that was within me and somehow, I had to walk into it to connect with my own inner peace. I arrived at a discovery of who I really am.

When I was 16 years old I had to move to the UK from Gambia and live with my brother and his family. At the time, I didn't know the language; I was only speaking French which made it difficult for me to communicate with the people here. As a result, I had to study English to enable me to get a job. You can imagine how hard it was for a 16-year-old coming to a new country, leaving her parents and siblings, having to adapt to a new environment and a different culture from her own. I remember how much I used to cry day and night because I didn't like it here; not having any friends to go out with; I was always indoors cleaning, cooking and looking after the children. That was my main role then.

Sadly in 1993 my Dad passed away; the man I loved so much; the only one I was able to communicate with had left me. From that day, I felt that I lost everything as I lost my friend and that same year I lost his two brothers whom were also my heroes because they were protecting me; but they had to depart too. I remember someone said to me in a rather horrible way that now they were gone what was I going to do as I had lost the people who always took my side. In my culture, I had been made an orphan and I certainly felt like one.

My self-confidence started to fade away, all my life I had lived it for others; believing what they thought of me. I never finished my education in The Gambia because they considered there was little or no use for my French education. It was decided that I simply had to stay at home. Previously in Senegal I used to get beaten a lot at school and at home whenever I did not know an answer to something. This led to limitations in what I could do or say even when I was right. This led to an insatiable need to always please people. I lived my life thinking that everything I did must be for the benefit and pleasure of other people. Mistakenly I thought that I was confident because of how I was in Senegal as a very young child. Back then I had lots of love, because of the love I received from my grand aunty who used to show me how to live life. She showed me how to value myself. That made me think that I had been given everything. Despite feeling that I had it all, I never really tapped into it. However; if I look back, I will always find the person that I was as a young child full of confidence.

I got married at a young age, having to adapt to a new life again to someone who I did not know. I thought I would do as I pleased when I liked. The reality was far different. I now had a new set of rules to follow.

One of my youthful pleasures was to get dressed up and beautifying myself, but even this was limited now and could only be done within set limitations. I thought I knew what life was all about and sometimes when I go back and look at that picture, the idea of such a happy girl, confident, full of herself being a Senegal Dakar girl.

I forgot that person and at some point, in my life, when I had all my children and felt sick with anxiety and depression, feeling sad, having experienced panic attacks almost every day, sitting on a sofa for the whole day; not being able to do everything I wanted to do for my children and submitting myself to taking anti-depression tablets and seeing a psychologist for CBT treatment. I no longer saw that happy beautiful young lady who wore those latest fashions.

Ramadan found us in The Gambia during our congregational prayer after breaking the fast one evening I collapsed. I was feeling shaky weird and breathless sweaty hands. Those around me collected me up and laid me on the bed. My feet and hands were cold and numb. I was unaware of what was around me except for the movement of people and the rubbing of my feet. I asked everyone's forgiveness because at that moment I thought the time of death had come. There wasn't any day in my life where I never think of dying no matter how much I tried to be happy no matter I do I couldn't be happy inside. Sometimes my husband would help and give me a bath that's how bad it was.

In those next weeks, I began to believe that my children were a source of peace and protection for me. Can you imagine a parent whose duty it is to protect a child feeling that, even for one second; that their child could protect them. Strange things were happening to me. I began to hear voices. One would tell me to leave my house in the middle of the night whilst the other said it was unsafe to do so. I listened to the one which said it was unsafe and did not go out. I used to have to call a friend and her husband would come with her and they would read Quran until I could calm down. I suffered with insomnia for many years I remember not sleeping the whole night and still function well day time, I would still laugh with people whilst I was dying inside. I did not understand where this was coming from. I prayed regularly and on time. I trusted that God was taking care of me. I believed that God does everything for a reason but searched far and wide for a solution to this issue. Some understanding into what I was going through.

Spiritual, mental and physical affliction

The thing that really benefited me at this time was my prayers. My attachment to God made it possible for me to continue. I would go to the hospital regularly with aching limbs and unexplained pains. I felt every day that I was going to die. Every day I pleaded with God to repair my broken body and would thank God for allowing me to wake the next morning.

How low can a person get to before being pushed into making a change? For me things were pretty low, it took the doctors 10 years to diagnose me with fibromyalgia a condition now recognised by the FBA as a depleting disorder with no cure. It attacks the nervous system and although it is suggested that its root causes lay within the psychological systems of the human the physiological effects are very real and very grave. The root of this sickness is caused by trauma. This continuous cycle meant that instead of solving problems I lost all my confidence. I did not know at that time, that this was the reason I was sick.

Even though at this point I had achieved much in education and had pursued a career in network marketing still I was not able to show my full potential. All the people around me could see something, but for me it was not there.

My children were seeing my inner power. They were seeing my peace and I know that I am a peaceful person. Yet something nagged at me, I could do better. I just did not know how. I had become stuck in that one place of pleasing everybody, traveling back and forth. Questioning myself pleasing others then reflecting and questioning again but returning to please others. The answer appeared always the same. My objective was to please others, never to please myself. Yet I did not want my children to think that way.

I had forgotten how to love myself. I had these deep-rooted fears. Fear had overtaken me. Fear of judgment. Fear of what others thought about me, fear had paralyzed me at this point.

I changed I took action, I chose this path, 2014 was my turning point when I realized that I either live or die. I had to choose one. I chose to find a way to fit my inner peace and lead with love for myself and for my children and the others. That's what god wanted me to do be happy and peaceful. That's when I knew that I could make a difference in this world, the moment that I took that journey to change myself. One day October 2014 my niece invited me to her house for a product launch. At the launch, she gave me aloe heat gel and rubbed it on my neck, shoulder and knees where I used to have tenderness, within 30 minutes I started to feel relief. The next day I could still feel the difference. I then call my niece to join me into the business. I have helped so many people including children who suffer acne, joint pain, chronic disease, Weight gain and conditions with the aloe Vera forever living products. I am so passionate about this company it's where wellness journey began.

My past is my strength and tools to guide people I found myself. The way I found myself is through the steps that I took. I would cry every single day trying to find myself before 2014. People would ask how, why? I've gone through so many things with my children. Life was upside down for us. But we hadn't struggled. We were a heroes and warriors to each other. They were always there for me. I was always there for them. Nothing could break us up insha-Allah. I've gone through so many things, but I was still firm and strong within me. I was still strong because I knew that all of that happened for a reason.

In 2015, I started going to personal development events. At this time, I was so much into my forever living business getting into supervisor in 2016 building customers and feeling positive again in life then June 2016 I became pregnant with my ninth child and going through social services involving in my family my life and the school, all were questioning me how I would manage nine children while my husband is traveling back and forth. This moment was very tough, but god has given the strength to overcome the situation, so we won as a team my children and I were very strong. I then began my journey again as fresh I started to do self-discovery finding out who am I and what kind of person do I want to become and for whom I do I want that for?

What are my strengths? What am I good at? What are my weaknesses? what am I not good at? how can I accept myself?

What knowledge do I have? and who can it benefit? Who can love me if I don't love thyself? I had to answered all of these.

I realised I couldn't change the people around me, but I was able to change my beliefs towards them and concentrate on my own self only then things can change.

I accepted all my childhood traumas and adulthood experiences, I needed to forgive and let go. Which I had to do between me and the ones that hurt me. I asked forgiveness from them to release myself from imprisonment.

I told myself that I am special god has given me talents, gifts and knowledge which is different from other peoples. I really looked deep into my inner self and assured myself that I am perfect in my imperfection way and I love just the way I am, and I had to believe it. Then I started acting just like that.

This is what made me really value self-love. I hold myself as the example of self-love. It took time and work because before then, I couldn't give to myself, everything I ever did, I did for other people. I didn't even buy myself a flower. I couldn't even buy myself chocolates. When I see something, I like, instead of buying it for myself I would always buy it for other people. This new journey has helped me to help look after myself. To value me, to really connect with myself, to find who I really was. This was so freeing and exciting.

Now I know how I am, I am a peaceful person. I love to help people. I love to make people happy. I love to do anything for people. However, I have now learnt, I can buy myself flowers,

I can give myself the love that I deserve. I don't care what anyone else says to me anymore. It doesn't hurt me because I know how to protect my inner emotions now.

All those things that used to make me break down and cry, it doesn't break me down anymore because I know the route to success, the route to walk straight without looking back and hold tight, and I decided to take that route, I decided that all those people that wanted to, or needed to come under my wings, to follow me along this journey we can all fly together. I know that's my vision that these people will be with me. They will travel with me and I think that my family, that includes my children, that includes my sisters. They are all with me now. They see the other side of me and now they like the other side of me.

I'm still the same person, but I took a different road, which will be beneficial for me and for the other people in my life. This is a truly beautiful journey. I suffered with so many things. But I now know how to tackle them. Right now, be able to talk to you, I know I'm helping so many people. I can serve them. Changing negative beliefs, removing trauma, past experiences, bringing confidence back to life, building your future, eliminate self-limiting beliefs through NLP.

I'm helping so many people through a 21-day process and 1:1. I'm helping so many people find their way back to self-love, self-confidence and to be fearless no matter what. The same way that I could help myself. Allows me to be able to guide those people that same way. I found the way to be the best version of myself, to love myself and be truly free. I got myself on this journey and I'm still on that journey because the journey never ends.

I want other women to know that they too have a voice, I want them to know that they have a voice and can use it. That they can speak out and use their voice. They just need to see the best side of life. They need to see the best version of themselves. They need to tap into their potential power. They need to tap into their inner peace and their inner power and put it all together and that will make the best life for them, it will be the best day ever!

I still say to myself as daily affirmations. That I am beautiful, I love how I talk, I love the way I walk. I love how I dress up. I must affirm all these things to myself. These are the things, the stuff that I must be so grateful for from my past, being grateful for the present, and being grateful for whatever comes in future. That is a project that I have taken and used to plant that good, positive seed back into me.

I first went into myself, that first step was tough I went in and I had to dig to find where that negative seed came from. Who planted it in me? It took time and I found that. This was a big lesson, I now know I must be aware of all these things and accepting them as their truths not mine. When I accepted that they have their own issues and thoughts, when I understood that I cannot do anything about it, I cannot change the other people. I learnt a big lesson, I must change myself.

I kept repeating my affirmations to myself between one and six times each day, saying these things to myself. How much I appreciate myself. How much I'm a warrior. And I called myself a warrior then because I had overcome this obstacle. Me. Myself, I had to do it.

I've listened to different motivational speakers and everything connects back to you. Now I must give myself back that strength.

I'm so happy that I can change me. My children as well. Now I have more connection with them. They're understanding what I'm doing more. And they get more benefits from it because I'm teaching them as well. They are seeing the different side that is in me, and it's so beautiful.

I see their challenges within them, I see how hard it is for them to accept themselves. I see how much they are lacking in confidence, that lack of self-esteem. Almost that they are looking for validation from other people rather than from their own selves. This is why I love to help. You can't look for validation from other people. Even me as your mother, don't look for validation from me. You look for it from your own self.

It's something that I see in children and teenagers, they are already suffering from this. I want them to hold onto what they've already got, hold onto their self-confidence, to realize and understand that everything they need is already within them. They just need some guidance. Most children right now are suffering because of what their parents are planting in them.

I know that as a parent. With the negatives that we inadvertently planted inside our children, they often do not realize that something is causing great pain inside them.

I recognize this because I'm the mother of nine beautiful children and I know that my life is a journey with my children. I feel even more assured that I must help my children through negative emotions. The amazing thing is every time that I talk to teenagers, it's like I'm here in front of my story from me and my children. Am a tree of different branches that different stories with different meanings. I believed my life holds many resources and tools.

I've never been so happy and fulfilled in my life. I've never been so content in my life. I'm so grateful for finding this journey. Finding these steps to finding myself. Finding these steps for my children because one of my daughters, she was supposed to deliver a speech at school, and she was feeling nervous.

One day, the day that she was going to go to do the speech, she said to me "Mommy, I want you to help me". Wow, she nailed it. Everybody was like "are you a speaker?" She's like "no, my mom is a speaker". She taught me. It's amazing and now my eldest son wants to do the same, it's been an amazing journey, and I am so truly grateful for this journey.

"I am good enough just the way I am".

MARK HARRIS

The Queen of self-love.

CEO of fkb inner peace academy transformational life/wellness coach, NLP practitioner and an international speaker relationships coaching. Mother of 9 beautiful children specialising in helping women and youths who are in total darkness in their life and don't know which road to take and get to that light. Finding it hard to know where to begin the search. These are people who suffer from anxiety, depression, which sometimes lead to lack of self-love, low self-esteem, fear of change suffers from chronic pain. Suffering from fibromyalgia and women who lose their whole self-worth. I help them tap into their inner power and lite the light and reconnect their inner peace, I give direction to empower themselves and bring confidence back and overcoming fear, through NLP techniques and strategies that will help to discover your true version of yourself. I am really passionate about helping people gaining their self-esteem to become the best version of themselves whilst using strategies to heal and transform and get a front row seat.

I was this person before and these were the techniques and strategies that helped me find my true self and become the #Queen of self-love. I now live the life I deserve and helped

1000 of people reconnect with their inner peace and self-love. The journey still carried on.

Fatou Kassama-Bayo

YouTube / LinkedIn Fatou Kassama-bayo
Email:info@fkbinnerpeaceacademy.com
www.fkbinnerpeaceacademy.com

9

Life A Blessing In Disguise

After leaving the children home I was feeling lost and confused by being placed there by someone I loved... I was a painter and decorator and had to leave my career when a crazy incident happened to me which changed my life.

I was racially attacked in Tenerife and beaten to near death. What happened next was unbelievable to me, and many others. There was a lady who saw the incident, someone who I never knew. As I was being beaten, lying unconscious on the floor, this stranger laid on top of me to protect me from further injuries. I was taken to hospital and when I came out of surgery and regained consciousness, I found out that the attackers also injured her, however her brave intervention saved my life. Today, that woman is my wife. My biggest challenges to date are that I am too giving of my heart, being too involved in trusting people and thinking that people are genuine, just like I am. I have learnt the hard way, when you wear your heart on your sleeve, it can sometimes be crushed. These were the same feelings I had when I left the children's home.

I had overcome all the hurt and the pain by listening to people who had (and still do) taken me underneath their wings. I have had some truly amazing people advising me where to go, encouraging me as to what I need to do to help myself, so that I can also help others too.

I'd never cried. I held all the painful experiences in my life inside of me for many years. When I did finally cry, I felt so free and at peace with myself (as you know some people say, "men don't cry").

I can recall the day that my life changed (big time). On my first personal development event, paid by a friend who saw something in me, I paired up with a complete stranger. Part of the course was to undertake an exercise, which was to look into each other's eyes and call upon an emotion. As I looked, I saw, I felt, and I heard all the hurt and pain coming back to me that I had experienced. The person who I was paired up with David (now a great friend) saw my eyes and started to cry. Seeing David's tear and the emotion that I saw in him, made me breakdown.

This was the first time that I had cried in 25 years. All my emotions came out. Aching. Discomfort. Pain. All this related to being abandoned from a young age, being made homeless at 17 and Tenerife.

The things that I faced that day after confronting the man in the mirror have been amazing. Learning to understand, believe and trust in others was a real deep thing for me. Within my life, I had always experienced that let down feeling.

The new dream life for me is to continue learning, improving and sharing the joys within, as we all are growing wiser and stronger together each and every day. I now want to make a difference to people lives and to help them release the emotional burdens within. As I close my eyes I can see the future, helping peers and sharing the stories that I told myself to assist, support and resonate with individuals. Inside of me I have this belief that if you save one, you can save many and now it's for me to help to use my experience and learning to guide others to find their truths. It's like a ripple effect. Throw the stone and watch the energy flow.

We all need guidance. We all need to make some sort of investment in ourselves. For me, in life we learn about everything and everybody else. Who taught you about you? We all need that person to be there as mentor, encourager, listener, friend or supporter to bring out the best in us.

Finding that person who makes a difference within people's lives would be amazing, as I have come to realize. Money can't buy authentic mind-sets. Invest in yourself and learn about you as you are unique, and you have an awesome part to play in this world. Continuously remember that you are remarkable, you can achieve whatever you want to in this world as the power is yours and that's the secret that has been kept away from you.

We are our own worst enemy, but my message to people is love with your heart, because everybody's got something to give. No one was born wicked or horrible. Everybody's got something for you. What you think you know, you don't know…. and what you don't know, you think you know.

What do I do now?
I have been a stay-at-home dad since 2005, raising my two boys; Isaac & Joshua. A true blessing to me.

Other inspiring work that I do is assisting in running two community centres working with young children and adults.

This has been my pleasure for the last seven years. I've coached people all the way through not knowing that it was called coaching. Now that I have found out what I have been doing naturally (adding value to lives) for the community makes me full of gratitude.

Coaching to me has been a gift, as there is nothing that can give me the joyfulness of someone finding themselves.

In my life, I was blocking what I was supposed to receive, through being bitter, twisted and angry within myself. Learning how to forgive has helped me realize what my true path was supposed to be helping, guiding and coaching others, but more importantly, setting myself free.

I personally believe that if you find yourself within the selfdevelopment realm, regardless of what you have done, you will discover how to be more authentic with yourself. I've forgiven my parents for what they done to me and through forgiving them, I now understand their journey. I've learnt that what I thought I knew, I never knew. Forgiveness is only one of the multiple keys to life.

Call/Email me to book your coaching session.

In just one session, you could:
- Gain control of your thoughts and feelings
- Shake off the anger
- Release the hurt
- Find peace of mind

Mark Harris

Forgivenesslifecoach@gmail.com

10

From Poverty, Drugs & Violence to International Speaker, TV Show Host &Spiritual Teacher

As I write this I can hear the waves crashing onto the shore of one of the most beautiful beaches I have ever seen on the paradise island of Maui, Hawaii. I am out in the US on the first leg of this year's StandOut World Speaking Tour, sharing my tools and techniques at events and through media interviews to help people manifest the life of their dreams. I feel truly blessed to be invited all over the world to share my message with people that are ready to wake up and take responsibility for how they show up in the world. I used to dream about being able to afford to go on vacations like this when I was younger; it seemed farfetched, but I somehow knew that I was going to break out of he pattern of my ancestors and could achieve anything that I truly wanted to. I have a deep knowing that every thought you think, every word you say and everything you do sends out ripples to the universe telling it exactly what you want from your life experience. Becoming aware of your energy is the first step to becoming a conscious creator. This is a lesson that I chose to learn the hard way. My intention is that my contribution to this book will give you the guidance you need to get to the next level in your life, without having to struggle and suffer for years like I did. Writing for me is a deeply reflective process and this could not be a better time for me to reflect on my entrepreneurial journey. I have just had the best performing quarter of my career so far, which essentially means I made more money in the past three months than I have ever made in my business before. I want to be honest with you that since becoming an entrepreneur there have been several months where I made absolutely nothing and couldn't even make my rent; I had to sleep on friend's sofas and rely on them to make me food just to survive. Being technically homeless whilst building up my business taught me a powerful lesson in leadership that I will share with you a little later. If you are like me and have that burning desire to help people; that feeling deep inside that you are destined for greatness; that knowingness that you are here to make a big impact in the world, then what I am writing here is specifically for you.

The problem is that the way our society is currently set up is not designed to encourage people to follow their dreams and to manifest their desires. Most people are deeply conditioned by their parents, teachers and friends to play small and safe in life and not to take risks or chances. Most of these people love us and want the best for us but they can only teach you things that they have learned themselves and unfortunately the vast majority of the world is very uneducated on the tools and techniques that you need to be truly successful in life. I want to be absolutely clear with you from the start that success to me is about much more than just money; success to me is about being free to choose how you want to live your life; success to me is about being able to live with integrity and in alignment with your highest values. Money is simply a form of energy that humans have agreed to use to exchange value with each other.

Having money doesn't guarantee that you will be happy, although your level of financial wealth can be a great indicator of what is going on inside of you. Everything that is happening in your outer world is a direct reflection of what is going on in your inner world.

I chose a very interesting start to life in this incarnation. My mum and dad were part of a famous motorcycle gang, the kind that ride Harley Davidson's and wear thick, leather jackets with tattoos all over their bodies. Many of my family members and close friends have been diagnosed with mental illnesses such as Bipolar Disorder, Schizophrenia, Manic Depression and PTSD. The town I am from has very poor resources for mental health issues and as a result doctors tend to prescribe medications liberally causing unnecessary addictions; this results in many people becoming addicted to other things to such as drugs, alcohol, sex and violence. Growing up in this kind of environment made it easy for me to find myself addicted to all these things and in a deep state of depression; completely lost, with no idea of how to get useful support as I had seen the westernised UK medical system fail to help any of my family and friends. My dad was addicted to drugs and battled with mental illness and whenever he became manic they would section him to a psychiatric hospital. My parents separated when I was a baby due to the drug addiction and my mum raised me and my brother on government benefits. In retrospect I am very grateful for all these experiences as I am now in a unique position to be able to guide and support people from all walks of life. This start to life provided me with a lot of contrast; it showed me what I didn't want for my future family and pushed me to excel in everything that I committed myself to.

Against the odds, something magical happened to me as a child with all this madness going on around me and with these circumstances stacked up against me; I had an unwavering belief that I was destined for greatness. I remember as a fiveyear-old being asked what I wanted to be when I was older, most boys said a fireman or a policeman, I said I wanted to be a millionaire! I was a very intelligent and gifted kid and at this young age created a plan that would then shape the rest of my life. I decided that I would get the best grades in school, go to a top university and own my own businesses. I loved to read and practically lived in the library. This was my safe place where I could escape reality and live my dreams. I became aware of self-made millionaires like Richard Branson and Alan Sugar and started to research them. It was like I was being guided to my purpose. I wanted to be a businessman!

Entrepreneurs are respected, they are powerful, and they can do whatever they want to do. I will become an entrepreneur! I started my first business around age six with my younger brother as my first employee, washing the cars of our neighbours on our street. I would handle the sales and my brother would do most of the labour. Our customer service was terrible, but we were cute and very reasonably priced, so we got away with it! This then lead to organising jumble sales on the corner of our street; selling off the neighbours unwanted items to passers-by. Our neighbours were happy to get rid of their junk and we would make a tidy profit! Genius!

Over the next 10 to 15 years I very much stuck to the plan made by five-year-old Luke. I graduated from one of the UK's top universities with a degree in Entrepreneurship and continued to build more and more businesses. When I was 19 I started my own ironing shop and had five employees. In my eyes, I had now made it! I was a real entrepreneur. I did everything from becoming a distributor of antiques to buying wholesale jewellery and even starting my own speed-dating events business. I had my own network marketing business for 2 years and ran a door-to-door sales business. It didn't matter to me what industry I went into as long as I could turn it into a viable opportunity. I was in love with business, it excited me and made me feel like my life had meaning. I had found my purpose! Or at least I thought I had at the time.

After university, I was searching for what I called my "£1 million idea". That one big business idea that could grow exponentially and I would be able to scale. It had eluded me so far and I was reminded of something that I learned whilst studying the world's top entrepreneurs. 90% of businesses fail in the first five years. Of the 10% businesses that are 'successful' (meaning they haven't failed yet), 40% of them were started by people that had been Directors of other companies first. They learned the ropes in another company first and made their mistakes there so that when they started their own company they already knew what they were doing. I had a 'eureka' moment! I would go and become a Director of a large, global organisation so that I could learn how the secrets of how the top companies in the world work.

I took a temp job in sales at a $2 Billion company and worked my way up the corporate ladder. Over the next five years I would break all the records at this company and defy every limitation that they tried to put on me. "You are too young to manage a team.". "Nobody has ever done that before." "It will never work." Sound familiar? I was well used to adversity, so these doubters just added fuel to my fire. Within 2 years I became the youngest ever manager at this huge, global organisation and was managing a team of 10 sales executives with multi-million-pound targets. You can be, do or have anything that you want in this life if believe you can achieve it. Fast-forward a few years and I worked my way up to a senior management position, travelling the world working on huge global projects with companies like Deloitte and PwC, learning all the secrets of how they operate.

I had gotten to the stage in my corporate career where the next step was to start getting press coverage, so I thought it would be a great idea to polish up my Public Speaking skills. As I searched for training courses I got targeted for a one-day speaker training event in London. My intuition went crazy and I knew that I had to be there. I found myself in a room with hundreds of like-minded people; all positive, entrepreneurial and with a desire to make a big impact in the world. The energy in this room was incredible! The whole training was amazing, but there was one thing the speaker said that really lit a fire in my belly. He said that: "Everybody has a message, and once you find out what your message is it is your duty to share it with the world." As I heard this, my whole body shivered; I knew that I had to become a public speaker. I had only felt this level of excitement and clarity a handful of times in my life. There was zero doubt or fear in my decision, I was sure that this was the right path for me.

One of my biggest challenges as an entrepreneur has been to find the right product, service and message that I truly believe in. I have worked with hundreds of businesses and have seen that the ones that are truly successful are the ones that really add value in people's lives. The companies that have a strong vision and mission to make a difference in the lives of their customers. The truth is that every idea that I followed up to this point has added something to my entrepreneurial toolbox. I had to learn from all those other opportunities to make me ready for the businesses that I run now. Too many people procrastinate while waiting for the perfect idea or the perfect conditions to change their life. I want you to know that the most important thing you can do is to learn how to connect with your heart and trust its guidance. When you follow that divine inspiration, the universe will bring you everything and everyone that you need to be successful on your journey. My message has evolved many times and I hope that it continues to evolve. Perfection doesn't exist. When something feels right, it is usually right; trust and take action!

Another huge challenge for me in business has been consistency. There have been many times on this journey when I felt myself shift up to new levels physically, mentally, emotionally, spiritually and financially. These huge highs were often followed by very low lows. I would have my best sales month ever, then nothing for the next two months; I would deliver my most incredibly powerful speech, then lose my mojo for the next one; I would create amazing new partnerships, then would lose existing ones. I know now that the reason for this is that just like a lot of small businesses I experienced big growth but didn't invest in the systems and infrastructure to support this growth. At every new stage of growth in your business you need to upgrade your infrastructure too. The exact things that get you to a five-figure business are the things that will stop you from becoming a six-figure business. The exact things that get you to a six-figure business are the things that will stop you from becoming a seven-figure business. It took me a long time and a lot of expensive mistakes to learn this lesson so if you are reading this and are looking to grow your business then please do the following immediately.

FIND YOURSELF A MENTOR THAT HAS ALREADY DONE WHAT YOU WANT TO DO AND ASK THEM TO GIVE YOU GUIDANCE AND SUPPORT.

You cannot afford not to get a mentor. In my first year of learning public speaking I invested over £20,000 in mentors, courses and programs so that I could learn from people that had already walked the path. Within six months I was being invited to speak at events all over the world and was making more money in my speaking business than I had ever made before.

This is the fastest way to become successful at anything in life. If you want to become a great tennis player what do you do? You ask a great tennis player to teach you. So, if you want to become a great entrepreneur, speaker or author what should you do? I love being a mentor. It is incredibly rewarding and satisfying for many reasons. I don't want anybody to have to suffer unnecessarily if I can help to guide them through an easier route. You can learn from mentors in many ways depending on your level of resourcefulness. I find one-on-one mentorships to be the most effective and the quickest; events and seminars are a great way to learn too; you can also learn from online courses, books and videos. People often say to me that they don't have enough time or money to get a mentor. I want to share something that my mentor told me that changed my whole life.

THERE IS NO SUCH THING AS A LACK OF RESOURCES, JUST A LACK OF RESOURCEFULNESS.

Real entrepreneurs are not constrained by time or money. If you need the investment, go and find it; investors are everywhere. If you need more time, make it a priority or outsource your workload to your team. Get resourceful. Stop making excuses. In this connected world there is really no excuse not to be learning and expanding your knowledge base every day. I mentioned earlier that I would share with you a lesson in leadership that I learned while I was homeless and still building my business. I learned that leaders need to ask for support. You are only a leader when you are leading people. This means that you can't do everything by yourself and call yourself a leader. This extreme situation caused me to ask for support and in doing so I freed up a lot of my time and resources as my basic needs were taken care of and I could focus on what was important to me, creating transformational products and services that can change the lives of my clients. I believe that this is a lesson that all leaders must learn eventually. What can you start to delegate or outsource? What kind of leader do you need to become for your team to take these things off your hands? Until you figure this out you will inevitably be limited in how much you can grow.

Right now, my mission in life is very clear to me. I choose every day to work towards living the Grandest Version of the Greatest Vision that I have had for myself. I feel privileged that the universe guides me through visions during my meditations. When I started my speaking business I had a vision during a meditation of speaking on global network television programs and radio shows, promoting my new book. I hadn't written a book at the time, but this vision was so vivid that I believed it to be real and this started a chain of reactions that would bring me to hosting my own TV show within 6 months. The StandOut Online Show was born, and this gave me access to the world's top entrepreneurs and thought leaders. I believed that this would happen with every fibre of my being, I didn't know the how, but I trusted that it would become a reality and it did! I have also been shown a vision of me creating a platform that helps millions of people around the world to find their own message and then to learn how to express it clearly so that their tribes can find them. This is one of the reasons that I founded the StandOut Speakers Academy and decided to become a mentor to aspiring speakers.

If you know that you have a big message or gift for the world then I would love to here from you. Let me know how myself or my team can support you on your journey. If you'd like to know more about me then please check out my social media channels and websites. Just search for 'Luke Scott Speaker' or 'Luke Scott Mentor' and all my channels will come up. Please do send a message to my team if you feel a pull to work together in some way. I hope we can connect in person at one of my talks or events. Make sure to check out my TV show and online courses too.

We help our clients in all sorts of ways including Mentorship, Group Coaching, Events and Online Courses that cover:

- Finding Your Aligned Message and Purpose
- Personal Branding Makeovers and Expert Authority Positioning
- Becoming a Powerful Presenter on Stage and on Camera
- Building a Profitable International Speaking Business
- Getting you Booked on Speaking Gigs, TV Shows, Radio Shows, Magazines and Podcasts
- Creating Studio Quality Videos and Course that Make You StandOut
- Establishing You as a Professional Speaker by Setting Up Your Own Events

- Connecting with Your Self Physically, Mentally, Emotionally and Spiritually.

About Luke Scott

Luke Scott is an International Speaker, Television Host and Spiritual Mentor.

Growing up in a dysfunctional family, drugs and violence were a normal part of Luke's home and family life. Luke never fitted into this environment and knew he was destined for much greater things.

From a young age, Luke was fascinated with business, sales and psychology and has had many business ventures which taught him some essential do's and don'ts. Luke spent 6 years working for a FTSE 100 company learning the secrets of how the world's most successful companies and people operate. After having a deep awakening experience, Luke began an intense journey to discover who he truly is and what he truly wants. Luke now travels the world sharing these secrets from stage so that others can achieve true success and happiness without having to spend 10 years learning these things themselves.

Luke's main values are growth and balance. "We can have everything in this life that we desire, but first we have to find out who we truly are and what we truly want."

Luke Scott

www.lukescottofficial.com

See Luke's TV show at:
www.standoutonline.tv

Closing of the book.

So, what's the point?

Why has this book been made?

What are your key takeaways?

We are hoping you have taken lots of notes, each entrepreneur has taken a different path, faced different challenges and created a different outcome.

Which story most resonates with you and why?

We would love to get your feedback, hear your stories and journeys so far, come connect with all the authors at https://www.facebook.com/planttheseedFruition

Did you notice what all these stories have in common?

We all had goals and dreams much larger than our fear of failure.

We all failed at many things before we had our successes.

We NEVER gave up, we never stopped trying, we ignored the naysayers. We failed 7 times and got up 8.

Our why's and our determination was much larger than ourselves, we used our challenges, to grow, learn and help others do the same.

LAURA HELEN

This book is intended to show you the truth behind the journey, being an entrepreneur is not easy, it is not a get rich quick scheme.

It takes continuous effort, drive and determination, it takes many failures, it takes the ability to fail fast and fail forward, the ability to get up again and never give up!

Set a plan, create your dream life on paper, then dream and vision the life, then do whatever it takes to make it happen. You must lose yourself to find yourself, when you find your true self and become aligned with your true purpose that's when the magic happens!

You may have to try and fail at many different things to find what your true gift is, remember being open and willing to learn the things you don't know you don't know.

The fastest way to success is to learn from other mistakes, instead of making them all on your own, every author in this book has at least one coach, and is an avid reader.

All our authors have ended their chapters with ways you may contact them, if there is a story that resonates, a goal achieved that you too wish to achieve, reach out and let's get you closer to your goal.

Thank you for taking the time to read, enjoy and learn from our journeys.

We look forward to connecting soon.

From Best Selling Author, Speaker & Coach

GET RID OF THE EXCUSES THAT YOU BLAME ON YOUR KIDS & CREATE LIFE ON YOUR TERMS

WHY I HATE MY KIDS

LAURA HELEN

#1 Book For All Parent Entrepreneurs

WHY I hate my Kids

Get rid of all the excuses that you blame on your kids and create life on your terms.

This book shares the secrets of entrepreneurial families making it happen with kids. Life can be challenging, and even tougher with kids. Having kids does not mean the end, stop thinking it can't happen. You must go for your goals and live the life of your dreams, because you do have kids. Your why should be bigger than your excuses. We as parents will do more for our kids than we will ever do for ourselves, so stop making excuses and create life on your terms, not only for you, but for your kids.

Kids give you a whole new perspective on life and can see the beauty in everything.

If you have kids, this is a must-read book for the entrepreneurial journey.

For the first chapter free go to:
831designs.com/why-i-hate-my-kids rial journey.

For the first chapter free go to:
831designs.com/why-i-hate-my-kids

LAURA HELEN

Matthew A. Cybulski

After life's up and downs, success and failures, I found myself at a crossroads in life. In my mid-20's I had the choice of taking a chance on a dream of mine, but unfortunately, it never materialized, and again I felt lost, confused and uncertain about my future. I took an offer from an established local family business and spent the next ten years climbing up the ladder to a management and leadership position.

Once in leadership, it was a topsy-turvy relationship until realizing that "people don't care how much you know until they know how much you care." It was that bit of advice from my mentor John C. Maxwell that led me further down the leadership path and led to my ultimate decision to pursue my passion of helping others.

After taking a leap of faith on myself, my potential and my passion, I became certified as a coach, speaker, and trainer by the largest leadership organization in the world, The John Maxwell Team. I then founded the M.A.C. Coaching & Leadership Development Company and began to find my wings on the way down. It ultimately led to fulfilling a dream to publish and write my own book. My first publication became an Best Seller and remains in the top 10 to this day.

Helping others dispel their self-limiting beliefs, uncover their calling and moving them to action is like air for my lungs. For me, there is no greater feeling than moving someone in the direction of their dreams and inspiring people to believe in themselves. So, are you ready to become your best self?

http://www.macleadership.com
https://www.facebook.com/findyourplaylist

This amazing family tour the world helping families ReAlign ReConnect and Grow Together!

Parents of the Awesome Tegan Helen & Tyler David.

They have a fantastic coaching programme for families.

They are on a mission to help make families Important again!

Their goal is to help 50,000 families. Best Selling Authors and they hold incredible events for families. Reconnecting is so important and so lacking in society!

Facebook.com/foreverfamilyforeverfree for updates.

Book them to talk at your next event:

foreverfamilyforeverfree@gmail.com

Also, owners of 831Designs,

Publishers of bestselling books!

You talk they write, a done for you service.

High quality books and service.

Creating books with their You Speak, We Create service, allowing you 100% creative control, 100% Royalties and Saving you 90% of the Time.

831designs.com

Tegan Helen - Princess-preneur

Published Author and Speaker

Money for Kids

This book teaches kids and adults alike real financial education that you do not get in school! Learn these key principles to change your financial future!

The Power to Unlock Your Dreams

This book teaches kids and adults alike the power that is the Law of Attraction. How this can be used to create the life of your dreams.

Be Fearless for Kids

This book teaches kids and adults alike. How they can overcome their fears. How to be truly fearless and make an impact in this world.

Find her on Social media, Facebook, YouTube, Twitter. Have your kids join her 6-week coaching programme to learn how to set goals and take action to reach them.

Book her to talk at your event:

kidsgetlearning@gmail.com

Tyler David 5-year-old Author helping one child at a time.

Check out 3 Tips For Aliens on Amazon!

Many Thanks To:

David Herbert

Trevor Buccieri

Anna Garcia

Orion Brutoco

Cody Broderick

Farah Butt

Talal Sany Kawar

Fatou Kassama-Bayo

Mark Harris

Luke Scott

And Laura Helen for making this all happen

Thank you to all our amazing authors who committed to themselves and their content in assisting us to create this truly inspiring book.

Our wish is that you have enjoyed this book, that it leaves you feeling both inspired and empowered. Now you know what to do, what not to do and now you know for sure that it takes hard work, and that it is truly possible.

"Every overnight success I know took years of training and discipline to create"

"Knowledge that is actioned IS power, now that you have learnt what to do, and what not to do, follow their journey, follow your heart, follow us on facebook"

https://www.facebook.com/planttheseedFruition

www.ingramcontent.com/pod-product-compliance
Lightning Source LLC
Chambersburg PA
CBHW052318220526
45472CB00001B/170